Rhythmanalysis

Bloomsbury Research Methods
Edited by Graham Crow and Mark Elliot

The Bloomsbury Research Methods series provides authoritative introductions to a range of research methods which are at the forefront of developments in a range of disciplines.

Each volume sets out the key elements of the particular method and features examples of its application, drawing on a consistent structure across the whole series. Written in an accessible style by leading experts in the field, this series is an innovative pedagogical and research resource.

Also available in the series

Community Studies, Graham Crow
Diary Method, Ruth Bartlett and Christine Milligan
GIS, Nick Bearman
Inclusive Research, Melanie Nind
Qualitative Longitudinal Research, Bren Neale
Quantitative Longitudinal Data Analysis, Vernon Gayle and Paul Lambert

Forthcoming in the series

Embodied Inquiry, Jennifer Leigh and Nicole Brown
Statistical Modelling in R, Kevin Ralston, Vernon Gayle, Roxanne Connelly and Chris Playford

Rhythmanalysis

Research Methods

Dawn Lyon

BLOOMSBURY ACADEMIC
LONDON • NEW YORK • OXFORD • NEW DELHI • SYDNEY

BLOOMSBURY ACADEMIC
Bloomsbury Publishing Plc
50 Bedford Square, London, WC1B 3DP, UK
1385 Broadway, New York, NY 10018, USA

BLOOMSBURY, BLOOMSBURY ACADEMIC and the Diana logo are trademarks of Bloomsbury Publishing Plc

First published Open Access under a Creative Commons license in 2019 as *What is Rhythmanalysis?*, this title is now also available as part of the Bloomsbury Research Methods series.
This edition published 2021

Copyright © Dawn Lyon, 2019, 2021

Dawn Lyon has asserted her right under the Copyright, Designs and Patents Act, 1988, to be identified as Author of this work.

For legal purposes the Acknowledgements on p. ix constitute an extension of this copyright page.

Series design by Charlotte James
Cover image © shuoshu / iStock

All rights reserved. No part of this publication may be reproduced or transmitted in any form or by any means, electronic or mechanical, including photocopying, recording, or any information storage or retrieval system, without prior permission in writing from the publishers.

Bloomsbury Publishing Plc does not have any control over, or responsibility for, any third-party websites referred to or in this book. All internet addresses given in this book were correct at the time of going to press. The author and publisher regret any inconvenience caused if addresses have changed or sites have ceased to exist, but can accept no responsibility for any such changes.

A catalogue record for this book is available from the British Library.

Library of Congress Cataloging-in-Publication Data

Names: Lyon, Dawn, author.
Title: Rhythmanalysis : research methods / Dawn Lyon.
Other titles: What is rhythmanalysis?
Description: London ; New York : Bloomsbury Academic, [2021] | Series: Bloomsbury research methods | "First published in 2019 as What is Rhythmanalysis?"–Colophon. | Includes bibliographical references and ndex.
Identifiers: LCCN 2020034772 (print) | LCCN 2020034773 (ebook) | ISBN 9781350188891 (hardback) | ISBN 9781350188907 (paperback) | ISBN 9781350188921 (ebook) | ISBN 9781350188914 (epub)
Subjects: LCSH: Lefebvre, Henri, 1901–1991. Éléments de rhythmanalyse. | Sociology–Research. | Public spaces–Social aspects. | Culture–Study nd teaching. | Research–Methodology.
Classification: LCC HT110 .L96 2021 (print) | LCC HT110 (ebook) | DDC 301.072–dc23
LC record available at https://lccn.loc.gov/2020034772
LC ebook record available at https://lccn.loc.gov/2020034773

ISBN: HB: 978-1-3501-8889-1
PB: 978-1-3501-8890-7
ePDF: 978-1-3501-8892-1
eBook: 978-1-3501-8891-4

Series: Bloomsbury Research Methods

Typeset by Deanta Global Publishing Services, Chennai, India

To find out more about our authors and books visit www.bloomsbury.com and sign up for our newsletters.

Contents

List of figures and tables   vi
Series foreword   vii
Acknowledgements   ix

1   **Introduction to rhythmanalysis**   1

2   **The history and development of rhythmanalysis: From Lefebvre to the present day**   19

3   **Key methodological orientations in doing rhythmanalysis: The body as central, displaced or insufficient**   45

4   **What is rhythmanalysis good for? Some gains, limitations and future directions of the rhythmanalytical project**   79

5   **What is rhythmanalysis? Conclusions**   95

References   105
Index   122

List of figures and tables

Images

Image 1.1   Sybil Andrews, *Rush Hour*, 1930, linocut on paper, EP 1, Collection of Glenbow; bequest of Sybil Andrews, 1995. Image copyright the Estate of Sybil Andrews, Glenbow, Calgary, Canada, 2017   10

Image 2.1   Rue Rambuteau 30 and 24, Paris 3^e, and view towards Centre Pompidou, 23 September 2017 (Author's own images)   29

Image 2.2   Tides, Isle of Sheppey, UK, 28 May 2017 (Author's own images)   42

Images 3.1 and 3.2   Seen from the coach window, inside and outside, 2007 (Tim Edensor, with kind permission)   52

Image 3.3   Stills from Billingsgate Fish Market, Dawn Lyon and Kevin Reynolds, 11 December 2012: https://www.youtube.com/watch?v=nw_kf32GfHY (Author's own images)   70

Image 4.1   Concertina journey by Tea, *By The Way*, 1999 (with kind permission of Peter Hatton)   88

Table

Table 2.1   Lefebvre's vocabulary of rhythm – summary of key terms   25

Series foreword

The idea behind this book series is a simple one: to provide concise and accessible introductions to frequently used research methods and of current issues in research methodology. Books in the series have been written by experts in their fields with a brief to write about their subject for a broad audience.

The series has been developed through a partnership between Bloomsbury and the UK's National Centre for Research Methods (NCRM). The original 'What is?' *Research Methods Series* sprang from the eponymous strand at NCRM's Research Methods Festivals.

This relaunched series reflects changes in the research landscape, embracing research methods innovation and interdisciplinarity. Methodological innovation is the order of the day, while still maintaining an emphasis on accessibility to a wide audience. The format allows researchers who are new to a field to gain an insight into its key features, while also providing a useful update on recent developments for people who have had some prior acquaintance with it. All readers should find it helpful to be taken through the discussion of key terms, the history of how the method or methodological issue has developed, and the assessment of the strengths and possible weaknesses of the approach through analysis of illustrative examples.

This book is devoted to rhythmanalysis. In it, Dawn Lyon provides an account of a methodological innovation inspired by the work of Henri Lefebvre, whose broad thinking is not easy to classify, spanning as it does several decades and many disciplines. His project of revealing the ways in which everyday social life is patterned by rhythms that in the normal course of things remain hidden has proved stimulating to researchers in fields as diverse as tourism, high-frequency trading, music festivals, social welfare in the night-time city, and everyday conversation (among many others). Rhythmanalysis is not like research methods that can be learnt and then applied in a more or less standard fashion, because it involves active engagement by the researcher with the rhythms under investigation, and the exercise of creativity in order to capture and then convey them. The diversity of forms in which rhythmanalytical research has been published confirms the centrality of this creative element, and Lyon's account conveys how new and inventive practices are being developed all the time. What holds them all together as a body of work is the researchers' commitment to the search for temporal patterning in social activity which may be missed in both the first impressions of a newcomer and the perceptions of a person with greater familiarity. The 'new science' that Lefebvre sought to found was envisaged like all sciences to be a means of making discoveries, and the record of research to date in this tradition that Lyon describes has repaid the faith of its practitioners in its potential to do this.

The books in this series cannot provide information about their subject matter down to a fine level of detail, but they will equip readers with a powerful sense of reasons why it deserves to be taken seriously and, it is hoped, with the enthusiasm to put that knowledge into practice.

Acknowledgements

Many people shaped and supported the development of this book. In particular I would like to thank Giulia Carabelli, Graham Crow, Tim Edensor, Steve Grix, Phil Hubbard, Ellie Jupp, Carolyn Pedwell, Lynne Pettinger, Chris Pickvance, Erin Sanders-McDonagh and Tim Strangleman as well as other colleagues at the University of Kent and anonymous reviewers for their comments, insights and encouragement.

1 Introduction to rhythmanalysis

Introduction: Why rhythmanalysis and why now?

There's a scene that has stayed with me from when I lived in Italy in the early 2000s. I would often pass a small grocery shop in the centre of Florence on my way to catch a bus to work early in the morning when the shop was first opening, or in the late afternoon when trade has resumed. State regulation stipulates the clock-time of operating hours[1] but this collective schedule also resonates with temporal norms of meal times and rest which leave room for the cyclical rhythms of the body, the household and the social life of the city. As I walked along the Via dell'Albero, I frequently saw a young man who was part of the family grocery business on the threshold of the shop talking to someone in the street – friends, fellow shopkeepers or customers it seemed – and I would also stop to say hello and exchange a few words when our paths and pace converged. The conversation had its own form and rhythm and shoppers were sometimes made to wait while it came to its conclusion. I can now see the constellations of rhythms that gave rise to these moments of coming together in time and space, on the street but not quite, the young man at work but sidestepping its totalizing hold, myself on the way to work but out of step with the day's trajectory in this encounter. The patience and accommodation of the shoppers feels important too; a collective refusal perhaps of the imposition of the linear rhythms of exchange and a tactic to retain a quality of everyday life that encompasses pleasure and meaning.

---

[1] Opening hours of small food shops are approximately 8.00 am–1.00 pm and 4.00 pm–7.30 pm, closed on Wednesday and Saturday afternoons and all day on Sundays. Exceptions to tightly defined operating hours already exist in tourist areas and recent legislation has extended flexibility. The impact of global capital, the demands of tourism, the presence of smaller units in city centres owned by supermarkets, and the readiness of migrant shopkeepers and workers to offer extensive trading hours in convenience stores are likely to lead to further change.

2 What is rhythmanalysis?

This book is concerned with understanding social life through the lens of rhythm. It emerged from my long-standing interest in how time and space are lived, produced, remembered and imagined, and how they shape the experience of everyday life as in the scene recounted above. Rhythm, it now seems, stimulated my curiosity beneath the surface in a series of projects in recent years. In a study of construction work, I was spellbound by the working rhythms of a man laying screed on a floor which he literally smoothed into shape through a combination of visual judgement and the graceful movement and pressure of his hands and body (Lyon 2012). And I can still bring to mind the sounds of fishmongers at work in a south London market as their gestures in chopping and filleting fish produced their own rhythm which could be heard all around – 'bang, bang, slice, pause' (Lyon and Back 2012). In these studies, I was interested in the reach and coordination of work across practices, people and things in time and space at different scales, such as the timing of laying screed in the refurbishment project or the sourcing of Caribbean fish to suit the tastes of the market's local customers. Rhythm finally came to the fore in my visual ethnography of Billingsgate fish market as I sought – and struggled – to identify the different coexisting spatial and temporal relations of market life. It was this project with all its surprising turns which prompted me to use and reflect on the potential of rhythmanalysis as a research strategy and a set of practices in the field (Lyon 2016 and see Chapter 3 for a discussion of this study). In this book, I explore what it means to undertake empirical research when attention to the 'flow and form' of rhythm comes into view (Benveniste 1966).

The intellectual starting point of the book is the work of the French 'philosopher cum sociologist, sociologist cum literary critic, literary critic cum urbanist, urbanist cum geographer' (Merrifield 2006: xxiv) Henri Lefebvre, and in particular his *Éléments de rythmanalyse: introduction à la connaissance des rythmes*, published in French in 1992, one year after his death and in English as *Rhythmanalysis, Space, Time & Everyday Life* in 2004. For Lefebvre, rhythm is always spatial and temporal and offers a means of grasping space and time together (Elden 2006: 186) and this remains its strength and appeal. There are many other scholars whose writings address rhythm in one way or another[2] but as far as I am aware, there is none whose

---

[2] See Henriques, Tianen and Väliaho (2014) for an account which highlights different contributions.

influence is felt so strongly in empirical research across the social sciences at the present time.

This book asks: What can attention to rhythm do for empirical research in the social sciences? What does working with rhythm as a tool of analysis – rhythmanalysis – offer? First though, what do we mean by rhythm? The *Oxford English Dictionary* defines rhythm as 'a regularly occurring sequence of events or processes' such as the rhythm of the tides. Equally, rhythm refers to a 'repeated pattern' such as in music or in language where there is a 'relation of long and short or stressed and unstressed syllables'.[3] For Lefebvre, 'Everywhere where there is interaction between a place, a time and an expenditure of energy, there is rhythm' (2004: 15). Rhythm requires repetition. But this is not enough on its own. Indeed, 'absolute repetition' is a 'fiction of logical and mathematical thought' (7). Instead, 'there is always something new and unforeseen that introduces itself into the repetitive: *difference*' (6, emphasis added).

Curiosity about rhythm on the part of scholars and social commentators has come and gone since at least the late eighteenth century as 'rhythm moves between disciplines' (Henriques, Tianen and Väliaho 2014: 4) across the natural sciences and philosophy, psychology, physiology, performance studies, literary criticism, law, sociology, anthropology, economics, geography and urban studies. At the present time, there is something of a resurgence of interest in rhythm in the Anglo-American academy in the social sciences and humanities.[4] This renewed awareness – or 'return' (ibid.: 3) – of rhythm can be seen in the context of concrete changes in the structures, processes, spaces and temporalities of everyday life and intellectual developments that lead to their perception anew.

---

[3] Oxford English Dictionary: https://en.oxforddictionaries.com/definition/rhythm
[4] In addition to the published work discussed in this book, there have been a number of recent events devoted to rhythm, including Symposium: Rhythm and Event (The London Graduate School, 2011): http://www.thelondongraduateschool.co.uk/blog/symposium-rhythmevent/ and http://backdoorbroadcasting.net/2011/10/rhythm-and-event/; Workshop: Rhythm Work (University of Nottingham 2014), Conference: Rhythm as Pattern and Variation (Goldsmiths 2016): https://audioculture.net/2016/05/25/audio-rhythm-as-pattern-and-variation-political-social-artistic-inflections/ and the CHASE seminar series, Rhythmanalysis: Everything You Always Wanted to Know but Were Afraid to Ask (Goldsmiths 2017): http://www.chase.ac.uk/rhythmanalysis and http://generic.wordpress.soton.ac.uk/rhythmanalysis/seminar/

There is some consensus that the pace of life in the Western world in the twentieth and twenty-first centuries has accelerated. Speed is the motif of the times and yet we have also seen the emergence of various slow movements for alternative ways of living – in cities, food production and scholarship. But there is more to this story. The experience of speed and slowness, motion and stillness, temporal autonomy and dependence is uneven and unequal between people and over time (Bissell and Fuller 2011; Hubbard and Lilley 2004; Sharma 2014; Virilio 1986; Wajcman and Dodd 2017). On the one hand, the time of professionals (lawyers and doctors for instance) is highly valued and rewarded, if also highly pressured. On the other, the delivery drivers of the gig economy barely have enough time in the day to get by financially while low-paid service workers on zero hours contracts find their needs for work and income out of synch with those of their employers. In addition, the temporal requirements of anticipation and presence – often 24/7 – in the work of the paid and unpaid care that keeps us all going are often at odds with rhythms that make for a good life.

While speed (and slowness) is often relevant for understanding the way we live in the world, it tends towards a linear spatialization of time and is too one dimensional to comprehend the temporal intricacies of lived experience. Thinking with rhythm offers a more multifaceted approach. It suggests a nuanced understanding of the articulations of tempo, movement, flow, stasis and repetition. And it advances a mode of analysis which recognizes different spatio-temporal relations and what they do in the world. In so doing, it illuminates the complex temporalities and territories of contemporary capitalism, it punctuates the lived embodied experience of the everyday, and it captures the imagination in making sense of the world across these scales.

Although interest in rhythm has gathered pace in recent years, the challenge of researching or analysing rhythm in the social sciences remains considerable. Lefebvre's *Rhythmanalysis* offers scholars a tantalizing grasp of rhythm but many readers have characterized it as an approach that stops short of being a method, arguing that he does not provide a systematic methodology for *doing* rhythmanalysis. Highmore describes it as an 'orientation' (2002: 175) for attending to the social world rather than as a technique for interrogating it; similarly for Hall, Lashua and Coffey, it is 'more an investigative disposition' than a 'method for systematic enquiry' (2008: 1028). Edensor thinks it is a 'suggestive vein of temporal thinking rather than a definitive methodology' (2011: 190),

McCormack characterizes it as 'a speculative invitation to think rhythmically' (2013: 42), and Borch, Bondo Hansen and Lange consider that it 'constitutes a rich reservoir of ideas for empirical work' (2015: 1082). The intangibility of rhythm itself may be part of the problem here. 'Rhythms. Rhythms.' Lefebvre bemoans. 'They reveal and they hide' (2004: 36). Or as Mels puts it, rhythm 'disappears' (2004: 23) as we attempt to get a hold on it. That said, there have been a number of studies and edited collections which have developed the practice of rhythmanalysis which are discussed in the pages that follow (for instance Chen 2017; Edensor 2010a; Mels 2004; McCormack 2013; Smith and Hetherington 2013; Stratford 2015).

This book in the 'What is?' Research Methods series addresses the task of how to *do* rhythmanalysis. It presents rhythmanalysis as a 'strategy of inquiry' which sits between the theories that inform a particular study and the specific methods used to collect and analyse data (Denzin and Lincoln 2018). So rather than being a method per se, rhythmanalysis comprises a set of methods; and these will vary according to the project at hand and the questions it asks. In this sense, rhythmanalysis has much in common with ethnography and it shares some of the methods used in ethnographic research, especially observation. However, it can also take other forms, including the more quantitative approaches used in the study of economic cycles or digital interaction.

This book critically discusses what Lefebvre and subsequent scholars have made of rhythmanalysis as a set of ideas and a research practice. It highlights the methodological choices and possibilities that can be drawn from Lefebvre's writings and subsequent studies through detailed discussion of examples. It explores the lively potential of rhythmanalysis for spatially, temporally and sensually attuned practices of research and for identifying and sensing different coexisting rhythms of everyday life at multiple scales. And it argues for rhythmanalysis as a promising, even 'instructive and inspiring' (Merrifield 2006), tool for empirical research into everyday life today. In so doing, it introduces rhythmanalysis to researchers who are new to it or who would like to reflect further on how to develop their own grasp of rhythm and make use of rhythmanalysis in their own work, especially in sociology, criminology, sociolegal studies, geography, urban studies, architecture, anthropology, economics and cultural studies. It also contributes to the development of apposite social science methods for the investigation of social life in the twenty-first century.

The remainder of this introductory chapter discusses the appeal of rhythm in historical perspective and situates Lefebvre's *Rhythmanalysis* in his broader thinking and politics of time, space and everyday life, before outlining the orientation and organization of this book. For readers who wish to jump ahead, the first part of Chapter 2 considers how Lefebvre conceptualized his rhythmanalytical project and sets out his key terms. This discussion is an important grounding for the rest of the book. It is followed by a review of examples of doing rhythmanalysis across different fields (in the second half of Chapter 2) and detailed discussion of three key approaches (Chapter 3). Chapter 4 offers a critical appraisal of what rhythmanalysis is good for in a discussion of its gains and limitations and Chapter 5 includes a worked example of thinking about a new project with rhythm in mind.

The appeal of rhythm in historical perspective

If 'rhythm returns' as Henriques, Tianen and Väliaho (2014: 3) put it, in what forms, times and places has it surfaced? There are many ways to tell a history of rhythm and its role in modernity in particular.[5] Here I restrict my focus to strands of thinking and practice in the social sciences and humanities that were either present in or parallel to the development of Lefebvre's ideas.

In the late nineteenth and early twentieth centuries, rhythm attracted considerable interest and even became a 'fetishized keyword of modernism' (Cowan 2012: 18–19 in Henriques, Tianen and Väliaho 2014: 7). This period was marked by significant shifts in the pace and reach of everyday life such as the development of mechanized transport and associated processes of industrialization, changes which gave rise to considerable anxiety and increased awareness of rhythm. The appeal of rhythm was in its capacity to capture the dynamism and fluidity of the times, and as a potential force for transformation. There are some interesting parallels between this earlier period and the global and fluid character of society and economy in the present day. Thinking with rhythm may have something to offer debates on the excessive pace of life and the attractions of slower living.

---

[5] Rhythm has a longer history than in modernity, dating at least from ancient and classical Greek thinking – see Pascal Michon (e.g. 2016) for a broader account.

With a focus on developments in France, French philosopher Pascal Michon (e.g. 2005, 2011, 2016, 2017 and his *Rhuthmos* website[6]) offers an intellectual genealogy of rhythm through the work of Roland Barthes, Émile Benveniste, Michel Serres, Michel Foucault, Edgar Morin, Henri Meschonnic, Gilles Deleuze and Felix Guattari as well as Lefebvre himself. For instance, Foucault's *Discipline and Punish* originally published in 1975 is precisely concerned with social and bodily rhythms – Michon argues – despite not making any explicit reference to rhythm. The modes of subjectivity produced through the new legal and political systems he discusses were most intensively rendered in institutions such as the prison but were equally present elsewhere. In *Refrains for Moving Bodies*, British cultural geographer Derek McCormack's account of the philosophical and artistic underpinnings and influence of rhythmanalysis makes some different connections. For instance, the American pragmatist philosopher John Dewey (1859–1952) (who has since had his own revival) was drawn to rhythm 'because it offers a way of thinking differentiation in process' (a view also found in the philosophy of Alfred North Whitehead). Dewey and Lefebvre – despite his ambivalence towards pragmatism – embraced the 'promise of rhythm as a corporeal and conceptual nexus through which to grasp the spacetimes in which bodies participate'. For both, rhythm is not just temporal but is something which *'takes place'* as Dewey puts it. This makes aesthetic experience possible and carries an ethical imperative: to multiply possibilities for living individually and collectively 'by making more of the expressive qualities generated by rhythmic spacetimes' (McCormack 2013: 40–1, emphasis in original).

These philosophical ideas were linked to efforts to cultivate rhythmic thinking or awareness through movement as 'a utopian vehicle' towards more authentic ways of life from the early twentieth century in the context of industrialization. *Eurhythmics*, developed by Émile Jaques-Dalcroze (1865–1950), was extremely popular across Europe, Russia and the United States, on a par with tango (Morris 2017: 52). It taught participants to increase conscious control over corporeal rhythms and complex bodily movements and develop an enhanced capacity for listening (*solfège*). For Jaques-Dalcroze, this training laid the foundations for fostering more experimental rhythms although contemporary commentators were more sceptical especially in relation to the troubling connections

[6] *Rhuthmos*: http://rhuthmos.eu/

between Jaques-Dalcroze's body politics and the political choreographies of German fascism (McCormack 2013: 40, 45–7, 52). Along with Jaques-Dalcroze, Rudolf Laban (1879–1958), a choreographer now well known for his *Labanotation* for the representation of movement,[7] and Rudolf Bode (1881–1970), a student of Jaques-Dalcroze who developed 'rhythmic gymnastics', were both fellow members of the 'Rhythmus movement' in Germany in the 1920s (Karina and Kant 2004: 66 in Crespi 2014: 34). While they agreed that rhythm was experienced at a corporeal level, Bode conceived of it as irrational and undivided whereas Laban considered it as polyrhythmic and polymorphous and their methodologies for rhythmanalysis were also at odds with one another (Laban 2014[1921], Crespi 2014: 341). Notwithstanding the uncomfortable political associations of the practices of all three of these figures and their differences in approach, the development of conscious kinaesthetic awareness of the effects of rhythm remains crucial in movement and performance (dance and theatre) in the twenty-first century (see Morris 2017) and turns out to be useful for today's rhythmanalyst (more on that later).

Important developments in the field of new media technologies also emerged in the late nineteenth and early twentieth centuries. In the realm of photography, Eadweard Muybridge (1830–1904) was something of a celebrity for his image-sequences of galloping horses and other animals in motion and his claims for the revelatory power of the camera. While Muybridge's sequences made motion visible, it was the French physiologist and Muybridge's contemporary, Étienne-Jules Marey (1830–1904), who contributed most to the scientific effort to dissemble time in space. Recognizing that, unaided, the senses failed to capture the complexity of action, through his 'chronophotography' (time-writing or photography of time) he literally made the trajectory of action apparent (Creswell 2006: 78; Miller 2010: 41). Cinema's capacity for further portraying speed and movement in time and space gave rise to new experiences of intensity and rhythm.

Photography was central to what later became known as time and motion studies, associated with the 'scientific management' of Frederick Taylor. In the 1910s and 1920s in the United States and later in Europe,[8] Taylorism,

---

[7] Laban dance centres were founded in the UK and New York.
[8] Similar ideas about time and rhythm were present in Soviet Russia (Henriques, Tianen and Väliaho 2014: 14).

as it was also known, was concerned with the 'rhythmic performance' of body and machine in newly established factories and industrial processes. Equipped with a stopwatch and his powers of observation, Taylor relied on his eye and the measure of the clock in his time studies which sought to control the working body in relation to contemporary ideals of 'new kinds of ruthlessly efficient mobilities' and a belief that rhythm was key to the successful accumulation of wealth (Creswell 2006: 83; Henriques, Tianen and Väliaho 2014: 13). In contrast, his collaborators cum rivals, Frank and Lilian Gilbreth developed more sophisticated means of analysing time and motion using photography and drawing and might be more accurately credited with the development of the field of time and motion studies (Creswell 2006: 99). Laban (introduced earlier) also turned his attention to the distribution and organization of 'effort' and 'appropriate use of movement' at work, notably for women. Towards the end of the Second World War, he collaborated with management consultant Fredrick Lawrence in the UK to develop the Laban-Lawrence Industrial Rhythm to improve bodily efficiency (Laban and Lawrence 1947; Creswell 2006: 125). Drawing on Taylor, he nevertheless differentiated his approach from motion studies through his emphasis on rhythm (2011[n.d.]: 232). These examples might retrospectively be seen as instances of rhythmanalysis (ahead of the term), if not progressive ones.

Changing relationships between time and space were also an important concern of artists and writers in this period. While Cubism reconstructed three-dimensional space, displacing any single viewpoint, Futurists incorporated sequences of action within a single image in their celebration of speed (and were directly indebted to Marey in their own photographic style). These and other artistic movements invoked rhythm to 'grasp the affective excess' of experience (McCormack 2013: 45). The British Grosvenor School of Modern Art 'adopted a Cubist-Futurist-Vorticist pictorial language' (Samuel 2015: 3) and one of its best-known proponents, Sybil Andrews (1898–1992), created animated linocuts that show the rhythms of everyday life. In *Rush Hour* (Image 1.1), the composition of the image brilliantly conveys the continuous movement of the escalators (Spalding 2014: 120) and, accentuated by the title, the recurrence of action across the cycles of the day. The viewer sees bodies interconnected in space but senses their movements as more fluid than in some of the machinic resonances of other works of the time. Rhythm was clearly at play in the imagination of the times.

10   What is rhythmanalysis?

Image 1.1 Sybil Andrews, *Rush Hour*, 1930, linocut on paper, EP 1, Collection of Glenbow; bequest of Sybil Andrews, 1995. Image copyright the Estate of Sybil Andrews, Glenbow, Calgary, Canada, 2017.

Finally, poets, playwrights and novelists[9] have long experimented with rhythm through language – as highlighted by one of the OED definitions of rhythm mentioned earlier. Two examples from the twentieth century indicate the capacity of language to evoke rhythm. The English writer Virginia Woolf (1882–1941) was an important figure in the literary world in the first decades of the twentieth century, prominent in London's Bloomsbury set of intellectuals, writers and artists. According to Adam Barrows she was 'one of the most rhythm-conscious prose writers in the English language' and a 'rhythmic reading of her work' reveals her characters 'as implicated in the global by means of their rhythmic interactions'. Rhythms are central to Woolf's project in her experimental novel *The Waves* based on subjective monologues in six voices (and notoriously difficult to read). Here she exemplifies the relationship between the corporeal and the global as she writes human tempos and subjectivity through everyday life into a broader material environment (2016: 62–5). The second example is the French writer

---

[9] I do not discuss musicians in this book although Lefebvre does have a chapter on 'Music and Rhythms' in *Rhythmanalysis*.

and film-maker Georges Perec (1936–82) who was in fact a student of Lefebvre, an influence that is clear in his attention to the 'infra-ordinary'. Perec was a member of the Oulipo group which famously devised literary constraints to trigger inspiration – his novel *La disparition* (1969) was written without using the letter 'e'. An earlier novel which he later made into a film, *Un homme qui dort* (1967), directly concerns the arrhythmic experience of wandering in the city guided only by bodily sensations, its proponents marginal but free in their refusal of the urban paths made for them (Villneuve 2008: 176–8).

Fast forward to the 1970s. Michon (e.g. 2011) argues that this decade witnessed the re-emergence of an interest in rhythm when structuralism and social stability were unsettled – a position Yi Chen (2017) echoes. An important contemporary development to consider as part of this contextualization of the appeal of rhythm is the time-geography of Swedish geographer Torsten Hägerstrand (1970) at the University of Lund who from the 1960s developed a system of notation and diagrammatic representations of movement in time and space. The novelty of Hägerstrand's work was to explicitly link space and time, for instance in research into diffusion in the spread of technologies and migration based initially on quantitative modelling and statistical techniques. This form of time-geography was criticized, not least by feminist scholars, as a rather rigid descriptive representation that was remote from everyday embodied experience (e.g. Rose 1993). Crang (2001) and later Edensor nevertheless identify Hägerstrand's time-geography as an important antecedent of rhythmanalysis. Edensor argues that Lefebvre's rhythmanalysis offers a 'fuller, richer analysis of these synchronic practices in space whilst also accounting for spatial qualities, sensations and intersubjective habits' (2010a: 2) and has sought to demonstrate this in his own work (discussed in Chapter 3). Lefebvre brings the body back into theoretical and empirical research on space and time and proposes a conceptual, practical and sensory grasp of space and time together which recognizes time space as produced in practice – and this is what makes rhythmanalysis so worth exploring today.

Situating *Rhythmanalysis* in Lefebvre's spatial politics and critique of everyday life

Henri Lefebvre was alive for most of the twentieth century – from 1901 to 1991 – and his thinking is as broad as the social, political, economic and cultural changes he witnessed, and often lamented. His start in life was in

12   What is rhythmanalysis?

the hamlet of Hagetmau in the foothills of the Pyrenees in southwest France where he was raised a Catholic. He would subsequently spend summer vacations close by in Navarrenx where his mother's family originated, and he returned there for military service and in retirement. His home region was also the subject of his early interest in agrarian and cyclical ways of living, the appeal of which remained with him and significantly informed his work. Rural life retained a certain authenticity and humanity for Lefebvre and was in tune with the rhythms of nature and the seasons. These connections were being eroded by the fragmentation and alienation of the industrialized consumerist society of contemporary France he saw taking shape. Trained in classical philosophy – gaining a degree at the age of seventeen – Lefebvre was dissatisfied with its 'relentless abstraction away from lived social relations'. The study of everyday life – with the help of Marx and Heidegger – kept his feet firmly on the ground (Alvarez 2007: 53–5).

Lefebvre's early working life was varied including military service – and time in the Resistance to Nazi occupation – factory and media work, teaching, and driving a Paris taxi (Elden 2004a: 2; Alvarez 2007: 52). He was sixty when he was appointed to the first chair in applied sociology in France at the University of Strasbourg in 1961 after working for most of the 1950s at different research centres in Paris. Over the previous decades, he had had a rocky relationship with the French Communist Party (PCF) which he joined in 1928 and from which he was suspended and then finally left thirty years later – a longer-lasting involvement than many of his contemporaries. However, free from the restrictions imposed by the party, he relished the opportunity to speak openly and gathered a large student following in Strasbourg and later Nanterre to the west of Paris. Theory and practice were inseparable for Lefebvre making politics part of his everyday and he is recognized (by some) as an important figure behind the 1968 student protests. He was involved with, influenced and was influenced by many of the key movements and groups of the second half of the twentieth century including Maoists, Situationists, notably founding member Guy Debord, and the CoBrA group of architects, especially Constant Nieuwenhuys who also shaped his interest in the urban (Elden 2004a: 3; Merrifield 2006: 33; Ross 1997: 70).[10]

---

[10] Lefebvre also recounts that it was a direct experience of 'brutal urbanization' that shifted his attention to the urban: 'One bright day, in my region, when bulldozers arrived and starting levelling the trees – they had discovered oil there' (Ross 1997: 76).

Stuart Elden argues that Lefebvre's work should 'be understood in the context of his Marxism and philosophy' and that his writing and teaching was always 'theoretically informed and politically engaged'. Lefebvre's was a humanist Marxism in contrast to the structuralism of Claude Lévi-Strauss and Louis Althusser. His analysis of the extension of capitalism broadened rather than departed from Marxism. He argued that alienation, as proposed by Marx, was not only a central concept for understanding the experience of labour in the formal or informal economy but that in the twentieth century it was relevant across all spheres of life including leisure and rest. Capitalism 'had increased its scope' in extent and form in a new way in the twentieth century and had come to 'dominate the cultural and social world as well as the economic' (Elden 2004a: 6, 9, 111).

Capitalism's colonization[11] of different spheres of life, notably through consumption, meant that it dominated what Lefebvre called *la vie quotidienne* – 'everyday life'. And this is a theme he wrote about at length in his three-volume *Critique of Everyday Life* (2014a) originally published separately in 1947, 1961 and 1981.[12] He uses the term 'everyday life' to describe the invasiveness of capitalism into routine practices, in other words, how lived experience is appropriated through ever more abstract and linear conceptualizations of space and time (Crang 2001: 201). Political, bureaucratic and commercial power seek to order rhythms in ways that are quickly habituated and undetected and thereby 'difficult to knowingly contravene' (Edensor and Holloway 2008: 483). The normative rules and conventions of social life often instituted by commercial forces and the state tell us what to do when, Power 'knows how to utilise and manipulate time, dates, time-tables' and to imprint rhythm in our practices (Lefebvre 2004: 68–9).

Yet for Lefebvre modern capitalism could never be 'seamless' and the 'level' of the everyday is also the site of revolutionary possibility (Merrifield 2006: 26; Lefebvre 2014a: 339). He sought radical change that would put an end to alienation, holding onto a belief in the future amid his darker musings

---

[11] In 'Clearing the Ground' in the second volume of *Critique of Everyday Life*, Lefebvre attributes to term 'colonized' to Guy Debord (Lefebvre 2014a: 305).

[12] Elden (2004a: 112) draws attention to the different meanings in French of '*quotidienne*' and to Lefebvre's own thoughts on its translation into English (Lefebvre and Levich 1987). While 'everyday life' is a fair translation of '*la vie quotidienne*', he argues, it misses the sense of the repetitive character of life that the French term implies, made more explicit in French as '*quotidienneté*' which can be translated as 'everydayness'.

(Elden 2004a: 117). The point of critical inquiry then was to bring about this transformation: 'The study of the everyday is not to be understood as literally documenting the details of life from one day to the next,' Lefebvre writes in the second volume of *Critique of Everyday Life*. 'Critique implies possibilities, and possibilities as yet unfulfilled. It is the task of critique to demonstrate what these possibilities and thus lack of fulfilment are' (2014a: 337, 312).

Rhythmanalysis emphasizes that linearity and standardization can never wholly capture either interior life or the patterning of the everyday (Barrows 2016: 87). This short work is often considered to be the fourth volume in the *Critique of Everyday Life* series. It demonstrates why Lefebvre was such an important thinker of the twentieth century within and beyond Marxism (Elden 2004b: vii). It shows how change occurs through the imprinting of new rhythms on an era (Lefebvre 2004: 14) and reveals how rhythms 'below the surface' are 'weighted with power' (Edensor 2010a: 8). As such, it offers potential for social analysis today and for thinking about new ways of living in the context of the social, economic and environmental challenges of the twenty-first century.

Orientation and organization of this book

While trying to do rhythmanalysis for the first time at Billingsgate fish market, my introduction to reading about it was through the work of Tim Edensor (2000, 2008, 2010a, 2010a, 2011, 2014) and Paul Simpson (2008, 2012) and I gratefully acknowledge their influence on this book. I have read and returned to the text of *Rhythmanalysis* itself to identify and develop insights and instructions for the practice of rhythmanalysis and have familiarized myself with some of Lefebvre's other writings. Since I was not a Lefebvre specialist, I am indebted to the accomplished scholarship of Stuart Elden[13] (2004a,b, 2006) and Rob Shields[14] (1998) in trying to get to grips with the range and significance of Lefebvre's thinking. The work of Andy Merrifield (2000, 2006) has also been a great help in gathering a sense

---

[13] See also Stuart Elden's Progressive Geographies blog: https://progressivegeographies.com/, notably, 'Where to start with reading Henri Lefebvre: https://progressivegeographies.com/resources/lefebvre-resources/where-to-start-with-reading-henri-lefebvre/ and *Henri Lefebvre, Key writings* (2017) edited with Elizabeth Lebas and Eleonore Kofman.

[14] Shields (1998) includes a comprehensive list of Lefebvre's writings.

of a man 'who wasn't afraid to philosophize on a grand, sweeping scale' in an astounding sixty or so books which have since been translated into thirty different languages (2006: xx). These and additional works (notably Butler 2012; McCormack 2013; and Stanek 2011) have alerted me to writings by Lefebvre that predate *Rhythmanalysis* and studies that have subsequently developed it, steering and opening up my understanding.

I have also come to this project as a feminist sociologist which means it has been a curious journey to spend so much time with the writings of a man who had little truck with feminist concerns. He had a patriarchal and heteronormative approach to the household along with a patronizing regard for the place of women in everyday life (Shields 2011: 283; Alvarez 2007: 72). For instance, while he recognized that everyday life burdens women more than men, he had no faith in women's capacity to realize and change their situations. His texts are littered with the casual sexism of the times – and an apparent reluctance to change with the times – and his personal life does not bear witness to any greater consideration of gender relations. Indeed, his own celebration of spontaneity and liberty left a string of ex-partners, ex-wives and children in its wake (Merrifield 2006: 17).[15] Furthermore, despite extensive travel and international connections in a life of politics as much as of learning, it is 'extraordinary', writes David Alvarez, 'that an anti-authoritarian thinker as attentive to world-historical circumstances' as Lefebvre should write so little about French imperialism (in Vietnam and Algeria) and the associated independence movements, or about revolutions further afield in Cuba or Nicaragua (2007: 72)[16] – although Lefebvre does mention risking dismissal from his post as a research director at the Centre National de la Recherche Scientifique (CNRS)[17] for supporting the Algerian cause (Ross 1997: 72). I would nevertheless argue that Lefebvre's project of thinking space and time together through rhythm can be deployed in a way that shakes off the sexism and other blind spots of its inception. As I will demonstrate, rhythmanalysis offers a way to analyse the complexity of space and time in twenty-first-century flexible

---

[15] Lefebvre had a total of six children with three of his four wives (Alvarez 2007: 52).
[16] Kipfer and Goonewardena argue that Lefebvre's notion of colonization 'presents a promising opening to understanding the "colonial" aspects of urbanisation today' (2013: 1). Lefebvre used colonization to understand the increasing alienation of all spheres of life through the dominance of linear over cyclical time (discussed in Chapter 2 of the present work) and in theories of imperialism in his work on the state.
[17] The CNRS is the national public research institution in France.

capitalism. Lefebvre's dual attention to the experience of embodiment in everyday life and the use of the body as a tool of research (see discussion in Chapter 2) offers powerful directions for researchers doing rhythmanalysis today wanting to recognize the gendered, classed and raced production of everyday life and knowledge about it.

This book is organized as follows. In this introduction, I have situated and presented rhythmanalysis in relation to the appeal of rhythm in historical perspective and Lefebvre's politics and thinking on everyday life. More generally, I have started to make a case for social scientists to engage with rhythmanalysis in order to better equip themselves to discern the multiple rhythms that underpin and matter for how we live in the twenty-first century.

Chapter 2 explores how Lefebvre envisaged and applied rhythmanalysis himself. It presents a close reading of his writings on rhythm and shows how his work continues to offer fascinating methodological perceptions and directions for researchers today. It sets out the rhythmic elements that Lefebvre distinguishes – linear and cyclical rhythms, 'polyrhythmia', 'arrhythmia', 'eurhythmia' and 'isorhythmia', and dressage. It critically discusses his argument for the centrality of the body in the practice of rhythmanalysis. The chapter then explores the uptake and development of rhythmanalysis in recent years, notably in research on place and mobility. This discussion offers the reader insight into studies of rhythm which 'extend the methodological inspiration offered by *Rhythmanalysis*' itself (Smith and Hetherington 2013: 10).

Chapter 3 focuses on three sets of examples which operationalize rhythmanalysis in different ways. The first considers the extensive rhythmanalytical work of Tim Edensor and how in collaboration with colleagues, he deploys the body as a key tool in the research process. The second considers the work of Christian Borch, Kristian Bondo Hansen and Ann-Christina Lange whose rhythmanalysis of finance displaces the centrality of the body as a research tool and offers insight into the everyday organization of capitalism itself. The third example is based on my own research on the workings of a fish market where the body is an important but insufficient tool of research. Here I present audiovisual methods as a means to document, perceive and analyse rhythm.

Some of the gains, limitations and future directions of the 'rhythmanalytical project' are brought together in Chapter 4. First, the chapter builds on discussion of rhythmanalysis as an embodied research practice and makes connections to methodological developments around the multi-sensory and material. Second, I critically consider rhythm in relation to other temporal concepts and discuss how we might better attend to conceptions of time in research design as well as use inventive strategies for playing with time in order to expose spatio-temporal relations. Third, it offers some reflections on the potential scale and scope of rhythmanalytical research; and in the final section, I critically discuss different means of conveying rhythm. Chapter 5 concludes the book with a worked example of 'doing rhythmanalysis over dinner' in the setting of an Italian restaurant. This imagined research is intended to reveal the questions and directions that rhythmanalysis inspires and the multiple ways researchers might orient themselves to be attuned to rhythm.

2 The history and development of rhythmanalysis: From Lefebvre to the present day

Introduction

A close reading of *Rhythmanalysis* offers inspiration and direction for researching (with) rhythm and the first aim of this chapter is to critically consider Lefebvre's thinking. If rhythmanalysis is a research strategy, how did he conceive of it? What did he have to say about the methods and research practices it implies? This chapter discusses the types of rhythm Lefebvre identified and how he advocated doing rhythmanalysis centred on the body. The second part of the chapter sets out areas where rhythmanalysis has been subsequently developed: in cultural history and studies of mobility, place, work and nature.

Foundations for rhythmanalysis: Lefebvre's 'moments'

Although not yet framed in the vocabulary he later develops, an important antecedent of rhythmanalysis is the final chapter of Volume 2 of Lefebvre's *Critique of Everyday Life* entitled 'The Theory of Moments', originally published in 1961 based on ideas he had previously introduced his 1959 two-volume autobiography, *La Somme et le Reste*.[1] Lefebvre was fascinated by moments of transcendence – what Griel Marcus calls 'tiny epiphanies' (1989: 144 in Shields 1998: 61) – in which it was possible to discern power and possibility. Moments are glimpses through time (past and future) unexpectedly illuminating 'a flash of the wider significance of some "thing"', writes Rob Shields. In the moment, there is sudden insight into the future which simultaneously recomposes the past (1998: 58, 59).

---

[1] *La Somme et le Reste* has not been translated into English.

This is fleeting: the moment 'vanishes, and at the same time it makes itself known' in a process of what Lefebvre calls *involution* as time 're-orientates itself like a curl of smoke' (Lefebvre 2014a: 636, 639; Lefebvre 1959: Tome I, 234 in Merrifield 2006: 28).

The moment is not the same as the 'instant' in philosopher Henri Bergson's terms (1859–1941). Indeed, Lefebvre was highly critical of Bergson's unbroken, linear and progressive time formulated as duration (*durée*) in which instants were points along a line. Gaston Bachelard (1884–1962) too had a more 'atomic' view of time and disagreed that Bergson's duration could be directly intuited. For Lefebvre, discontinuities open the way to revolution, and no more so than in the moment's rupture of the mundane. The moment is a 'primordial form of time' according to Shields, which breaks up the banality of the everyday (1998: 60–1). It is a 'higher form of repetition, renewal and reappearance' singled out or separated '*from a muddle or a confusion*'; in short, it is '*the attempt to achieve the total realization of a possibility*' (Lefebvre 2014a: 638, 642, emphasis in original).

For Lefebvre, moments offered important keys for understanding the everyday and for stimulating change. Among the many thinkers and movements in Europe he was engaged with across the twentieth century, Surrealism and especially the irreverence of Dadaism caught the attention of the young Lefebvre in the 1920s. He 'was transfixed by the potential of surprise, shock and humour for thinking of not only artistic images but of everyday life in new ways', writes Shields (1998: 54), although he was subsequently deeply critical of the nihilism of these movements. Some decades later in the late 1950s and early 1960s, he had a close connection to the Situationists – especially Guy Debord – and there are important parallels between Debord's 'situation' and Lefebvre's moment.[2]

Both Lefebvre and Debord were fascinated by the idea of the 'festival'.[3] For Lefebvre, also inspired by François Rabelais' 'excess' and his own early experience of rural life, the festival offers a 'moment' of escape from the relentless and oppressive linearity of modernity when 'its brilliance lights up the sad hinterland of everyday dullness' (Merrifield 2006: 17; Lefebvre

---

[2] This similarity and associated accusations of plagiarism was one source of the rift between them. See Lefebvre's account in an interview with Kristin Ross (Ross 1997).

[3] Rudolf Laban, a contemporary of Lefebvre's working in Germany known for his notation of choreography (as discussed in Chapter 1), was also interested in the festival for its intensification of the everyday (Laban 2014[1921]: 77). To the best of my knowledge, Lefebvre does not refer to him.

2014a: 650). In 'Notes Written One Sunday in the French Countryside' in the first volume of *Critique of Everyday Life* published in 1947, Lefebvre wrote: 'Festival differed from everyday life only in the explosion of forces which had been slowly accumulated in and via everyday life itself' (2014a: 222). So while festivals contrasted with the everyday, even 'violently', '*they were not separate from it*' (227, emphasis in original).[4] (A man of strong appetites, he embraced the revelry and excess of the festival in practice as well as theory.) Historically, the energies of the festival had culminated in the 1871 Paris Commune when revolution was rowdily inserted into the fabric of the everyday. And in his own lifetime, Lefebvre is partly credited with fuelling the student unrest which started in March 1968 at Nanterre and which in May erupted more powerfully still at the Sorbonne and on the Left Bank leading to a general strike by millions of workers and the occupation of workplaces in Paris and elsewhere in France. Everything stopped as the spirit of the festival took hold (Alvarez 2007: 61, 64).

According to Yi Chen, the qualities of the moment make it a useful 'optic for cultural analysis' today. In practice, the rhythmanalyst must show 'sensitivity to moments', pay heed to their vitality and capacity 'to maintain and transform the temporal-spatial structure of experiences' and reveal relations which are normally veiled. Patterns of recurrent, if diverse, moments produce rhythms; in other words, rhythms may be composed of constellations of moments, intervals and repetition (Chen 2017: 20, 21, 24).

The development of rhythmanalysis

Lefebvre's 'extraordinary impact in the Anglo-American academy' emerged following the publication in English of *The Production of Space* in 1991 (Elden 2004a: 5), largely thanks to Anglo-American geographer David Harvey who has continued to be an important figure in disseminating his ideas. The notion/slogan of the 'right to the city'[5] expressed in Lefebvre's 1968 book of the same name – published in English in *Writings on Cities* in 1995 (see also Butler 2012) – chimes with Harvey's own thinking in *Social Justice and the City* (1973) on the importance of a specifically urban revolution (Merrifield 2006: 102). Lefebvre's *Éléments de rythmanalyse: introduction*

---

[4] Rituals of rebellion can be understood as reinforcing the existing social order.
[5] Rather than an individual liberty, this right concerns collective power to change the process of urbanization, to remake the city and the self.

à la connaissance des rythmes was originally published in French in 1992, one year after his death. However, it was the publication of the English translation, *Rhythmanalysis*, in 2004 that reinvigorated interest in Lefebvre, giving him something of an 'afterlife', as Stuart Elden (2006) aptly puts it.[6]

The term 'rhythmanalysis' comes from Lúcio Alberto Pinheiro dos Santos (1889–1950), a Portuguese philosopher who was concerned with material, biological and psychological rhythms in a short work, *Ritmanálise*, published in 1931, although the idea had little impact at the time. Ahead of Lefebvre, it was the French philosopher Gaston Bachelard who discussed the contribution of dos Santos.[7] Lefebvre acknowledges both dos Santos and Bachelard's use of the term 'rhythmanalysis' despite their lack of development of its meaning. Through his own contribution he says, the rhythmanalytical project 'emerges bit by bit from the shadows' (Lefebvre 2004: 9).

Rhythmanalysis starts out boldly: 'This little book does not conceal its ambition. It proposes nothing less than to found a new science, a new field of knowledge: the analysis of rhythms.' This can happen in two ways, Lefebvre continues: we can either study and compare cases, in other words, focus on 'practice', or we can start with 'concepts', 'with full consciousness of the abstract in order to arrive at the concrete'. *Rhythmanalysis* follows the second 'more philosophical method', he clarifies, and it relies on broad interdisciplinary thinking which is characteristic of Lefebvre's work more generally (Lefebvre 2004: 3, 5).

> The rhythmanalysis here defined as a method and a theory pursues this time-honoured labour [the discovery of rhythms] in a systematic and theoretical manner, by bringing together very diverse practices and very different types of knowledge: medicine, history, climatology, cosmology, poetry (the poetic), etc. Not forgetting, of course, sociology and psychology, which occupy the front line and supply the essentials. (Lefebvre 2004: 16)

---

[6] Lefebvre's work has also been popular in Japan and South Korea. In France, there has been some resurgence of interest and the republication of some out-of-print books (Elden 2004a: 6; Revol 2012/3) but his standing is a long way from that accorded in the Anglo-American world.

[7] In *The Psychoanalysis of Fire* and more fully in a chapter in *The Dialectic of Duration* (2000), first published in French in 1936.

We might think of the rhythmanalyst as akin to the poet, Lefebvre suggests, insofar as both are concerned with the verbal and the aesthetic and both change what they observe. Indeed, Lefebvre previously suggested that rhythmanalysis could be effectively explored across the arts including poetry, music, dance and theatre (1991: 406). The rhythmanalyst is also similar to the psychoanalyst[8] in terms of the quality of attentiveness both bring to their task. On the other hand, the rhythmanalyst is less associated with the statistician he states, at least not one who counts and describes things in their 'immobility'.

Central to the rhythmanalytical project is a concern with 'temporalities and their relations within wholes' (Lefebvre 2004: 23–5). In addition to the 'moments' discussed in the previous section, we can retrospectively read how in his earlier writings, Lefebvre paved the way for thinking spatio-temporal relations in *Rhythmanalysis*. In a chapter on 'Spatial Architectonics' in *The Production of Space* published in 1974,[9] he suggests that 'it is possible to envision a sort of "rhythm analysis" which would address itself to the concrete reality of rhythms'. He highlights how 'rhythms in all their multiplicity interpenetrate one another' – in particular – in and around the body. Some rhythms 'operate on the surface', he notes, and are therefore easy to trace while others 'spring from hidden depths' and must be tracked 'through indirect effects' (1991: 205). Rhythmanalysis is further developed in a short section on 'Space and Time' in Volume 3 of *Critique of Everyday Life* published in 1981 – a full twenty years after the second volume in which 'The Theory of Moments' emerged.[10] Here, Lefebvre critiques the poor understanding of his fellow Marxists for their failure to recognize the rhythms of labour. He proposes the elaboration of 'a new science' that 'studies these highly complex processes' and is situated 'at the juxtaposition of the physical, the physiological and the social, at the heart of daily life'.[11] His approach 'starts from empirical observations' and makes use of what he calls 'spectral analysis' in which something apparently simple is refracted through a prism to reveal, however incompletely, its elements and history (2014a: 802, 804).

[8] Lefebvre previously stated that 'rhythm analysis might eventually even displace psychoanalysis' (1991: 205), or 'complement or supplant' it (2014: 802).
[9] Dates refer to the original publications in French.
[10] The second volume of his *Critique of Everyday Life* was originally published in 1961.
[11] Lefebvre is clearly indebted to dos Santos in this lack of separation between material, living and social bodies (McCormack 2013: 42).

Having outlined some key aspects of *Rhythmanalysis* in this introduction, the following sections now go into more depth. The first aim is to clarify Lefebvre's distinctions between rhythm and repetition, the linear and the cyclical, and to consider further terms in his vocabulary of rhythm; and the second is to critically consider the role of the body in rhythmanalysis.

Rhythm and repetition: The linear and the cyclical

For Lefebvre, the expenditure of energy that produces rhythm happens through repetition, interferences (across the linear and cyclical) and 'birth, growth, peak, decline and end' (2004: 15). Rhythms vary in their amplitude, energies and frequency producing different intensities of anticipation, tension and action (1991: 206). But the conundrum of researching rhythm persists. Although rhythms are part of our lives, they are not part of what we know, Lefebvre argues, and conceptually, 'the meanings of the term [rhythm] remain obscure' (2004: 5). In this section, I discuss key terms in the conceptual repertoire put forward by Lefebvre to undertake rhythmanalysis (summarized in Table 2.1).

First, rhythm requires repetition, Lefebvre explains: 'But there is no identical absolute repetition indefinitely.' Difference is key as 'something new and unforeseen that introduces itself into the repetitive' (2004: 6). This echoes his earlier formation in Volume 2 of *Critique of Everyday Life*: 'No return is absolutely exact. ... If it were otherwise, cycles would be vicious circles and the geometry of the circle would exhaust all that is possible' (2014a: 342). In *Rhythmanalysis*, Lefebvre refers to two ways in which repetition and difference are linked. Repetition *includes* difference in the sense that each repeated element is different from the preceding or subsequent one quite simply because it is not that one. And repetition *produces* difference as difference emerges from the very act of repetition (2004: 7).

Lefebvre places *linear* and *cyclical* rhythms at the heart of rhythmanalysis and in tension and opposition to one another. In Volume 2 of the *Critique of Everyday Life*, he introduces this: 'We will look closely at results of interactions between cyclic rhythms and linear (discontinuous or continuous) time scales in the everyday. Therefore we will be proposing a rhythmology or a sociological "rhythmanalysis"' (2014a: 526). In his early work, he reserved the term rhythm for the cyclical, and the linear was discussed in terms of repetition. However, later on, both the linear and the cyclical are presented as different forms of rhythm. He uses musical terms here to evoke the differences between them: whereas measure and beat are linear, melody and harmony are cyclical (1991: 206).

Table 2.1 Lefebvre's vocabulary of rhythm – summary of key terms.

Linear rhythm	Quantified and fragmented time, imposed by technology, industry and consumption
	The time of the city and urban life
	Closer to repetition than rhythm per se, for example dripping of water, the beats of a hammer
	In musical terms, measure and beat
Cyclical rhythm	The time of nature, 'cosmic and vital', evident in seasons and day and night
	In biology and the body, for example heart beats and eye movements
	Characteristic of rural life – cyclical rhythm is destroyed by capitalism
	Includes repetition *and* difference
	In musical terms, melody and harmony
Polyrhythmia	A multitude of rhythms; the effects of different configurations of rhythm
Eurhythmia	When rhythms combine smoothly, for example in good health
Arrhythmia	Discordance between rhythms, being 'out of step'
Isorhythmia	An 'equality of rhythms' beyond *eurhythmia*, for example in the coordination of an orchestra
Dressage	Process of bodily entrainment and repetition through which rhythm is learnt and becomes evident in the body over time, for example in military drills

For Lefebvre, cyclical time scales are linked to nature which has long 'held sway' over everyday life (2014a: 341). They comprise rhythms that are 'present from molecules to galaxies, passing through the beatings of the heart, the blinking of the eyelids and breathing, the alternation of days and nights, months and seasons and so on' (Lefebvre and Régulier 2004a: 76). From his studies of rural village life, he writes: 'The house, the field, the tree, the sky, the mountain or the sea are not simply what they are. Cosmic and vital rhythms envelop them, subtle resonances accompany them, every "thing" is part of a song' (Lefebvre 2014a: 601–2).

In contrast, the 'quantified' linear time of capitalism is 'homogeneous' and 'fragmented', 'monotonous, tiring and even intolerable'. Linear time is imposed by technology and industrial labour and concerned with mechanical gestures of accumulation. It 'designates any series of identical facts separated by long or short periods of time: the fall of a drop of water, the blows of a hammer, the noise of an engine, and so on' but these do not amount to rhythm since 'only a non-mechanical movement can have rhythm' (Lefebvre and Régulier 2004a: 76–8). It is Lefebvre's contention that the less-than-human linear time of modernity is taking over the natural cyclical rhythms of everyday life. Consumer capitalism commodifies and splits time and disregards what a lack of rhythm means for everyday life. It brings about 'lassitude, boredom and fatigue' – and perhaps burn out and breakdown.

The relationship between the linear and the cyclical is already made clear in the second volume of the *Critique of Everyday Life*: '*Critique of everyday life studies the persistence of rhythmic time scales within the linear time of modern industrial society*' and the '*defects and disquiet*' that arise from these interactions (2014a: 343, emphases in original). However, relations between linear and cyclical rhythms are not straightforward as they 'interfere with one another constantly' at times resulting in 'compromises' or 'disturbances' (Lefebvre 2004: 8). What Lefebvre describes as 'rational' rhythms impose themselves on the body's 'natural' rhythms and in so doing change them. These new rhythms become both rational and natural at the same time but cannot be reduced to one or the other (2004: 9, 12). Expressed more strongly: 'Rational and industrial techniques have "shattered cyclic time"'. They fragment time and produce repetitive gestures. Yet, 'cyclic time scales have not disappeared', he asserts. Indeed, they 'live on' in the biological and the social (2014a: 342). Institutionalized social rhythms from national holidays to television schedules and synchronized habits and patterns of work bring people together (Zerabuvel 1981). They are also intertwined with the rhythms of our bodies and those of the natural world, from light and day to the changes of the seasons (Edensor 2011: 189, 191). Lefebvre is often gloomy, but hope remains in the cracks and crevices in the everyday.

A vocabulary of rhythm

For Lefebvre, the world is composed of a multiplicity of rhythms and it is important to distinguish between the categories of 'polyrhythmia', 'arrhythmia', 'eurhythmia' and 'isorhythmia'.[12] 'The everyday reveals itself to be a polyrhythmia from the first listening,' he states, as we first attend to

---

[12] These terms overlap with those used by Laban and Bode discussed in Chapter 1 and *arrhythmia* is also present in medical vocabulary.

our own bodily multitude of rhythms (2004: 16). Yet these rhythms may coordinate or clash. When rhythms smoothly combine with one another which they often do, they produce a state of *eurhythmia* which he associates with the condition of good health. Conversely, *arrhythmia* arises when there is discordance between rhythms, such as occurs (biologically) in an unwell person. Finally, *isorhythmia* refers to the 'equality of rhythms' and these are rare, beyond eurhythmia – such as in the 'remarkable' coordination of an orchestra 'under the direction of the conductor's baton' (Lefebvre 2004: 68).

There is more to come still. *Dressage* is pivotal as a process of bodily entrainment which 'determines the majority of rhythms', writes Lefebvre (2004: 40), and the effect of rhythm as it constitutes the body in a particular way achieved through repetition over time. For instance, there are deemed to be 'proper' ways to walk and to hold the body in movement and at rest. Entering into the social means 'to bend oneself (to be bent) to its ways', and humans must 'break themselves in like animals' (Lefebvre 2004: 39) – presumably within processes of socialization which make this happen. While this is clearly relevant in military instruction, he says (see also McNeill 1997), it is equally present in everyday learning. This idea has much in common with Marcel Mauss' and later Pierre Bourdieu's notion of *habitus* for the ways in which the body is quite literally shaped in relation to the techniques, habits and practices of class, gender, ethnicity, nationality and so on. And it is echoed in the docile bodies produced by the disciplinary practices Michel Foucault identified.[13] Indeed, the embodied character of dressage means that we do not have to think how to act: 'Dressage fills the place of the unforeseen' for Lefebvre (Lefebvre 2004: 40). However, he also recognizes the contingent nature of this regulation. As he gazes from his balcony in the rue Rambuteau in Paris, he perceives the rhythms of tourists and city workers at odds with one another and with this the immanent possibility of their resistance.

Doing rhythmanalysis with and beyond the body

In his work on rhythmanalysis with his (last) wife and collaborator, Catherine Régulier, Lefebvre made it clear that in order to grasp rhythm

---

[13] Foucault and Lefebvre disagreed on the operation of power: for Foucault it is part of everyday practices which may or may not enhance the capacity to act, for Lefebvre it is always repressive (Kullman and Palludan 2011: 351). Lefebvre was also critical of Foucault's emphasis on 'systematized knowledge (*savoir*) at the expense of the experiential (*connaissance*)' as exemplified in their respective understandings of discipline and dressage (Stratford 2015: 10).

Image 2.1 Rue Rambuteau 30 and 24, Paris 3ᵉ, and view towards Centre Pompidou, 23 September 2017 (Author's own images).

a detailed description of the deployment of time is 'inadequate' since 'it captures the accidental but misses the essential'. The message is clear: it is insufficient to attend to the timetables of everyday life as to do so would mean being caught in a solely linear conception of time. 'The everyday does not consist in a series of time lapses, but in the concatenation of these time lapses: not their sum but their rhythm' (Lefebvre, Régulier and Zayani 1999; Lefebvre and Régulier 2004a: 8).[14] There are further challenges: 'Rhythm

---

[14] This phrasing comes from an earlier translation of 'The Rhythmanalytical Project' (Lefebvre, Régulier and Zayani 1999).

enters into the lived; though that does not mean it enters into the known' (Lefebvre 2004: 77). How then does one do rhythmanalysis? In this section, I discuss Lefebvre's understanding of rhythmanalysis as an embodied phenomenological practice.

Lefebvre lived for more than thirty years at two addresses, numbers 24 and 30 on the rue Rambuteau in the third *arrondissement* of Paris (see Image 2.1). Here he witnessed and lamented the destruction of the former *Les Halles* markets and the building of the Pompidou centre within spitting distance of his apartment close to the corner of rue Beaubourg (Merrifield 2006: 22). It is where he wrote 'Seen from the Window', the third chapter of *Rhythmanalysis* and arguably the centrepiece of the book, from which we can draw out his 'instructions' for doing rhythmanalysis.

> From the window opening onto rue R. facing the famous P.Centre, there is no need to lean much to see into the distance. ... He [sic][15] who walks down the street, over there, is immersed in the multiplicity of noises, murmurs, rhythms (including those of the body, but does he pay attention, except at the moment of crossing the street, when he has to calculate roughly the number of his steps?). By contrast, from the window, the noises distinguish themselves, the flows separate out, rhythms respond to one another. Towards the right, below, a traffic light. On red, cars at a standstill, the pedestrians cross, feeble murmurings, footsteps, confused voices. One does not chatter while crossing a dangerous junction under the threat of wild cats and elephants ready to charge forward, taxis, buses, lorries, various cars. Hence the relative silence in this crowd. A kind of soft murmuring, sometimes a cry, a call. (Lefebvre 2004: 28)

Reading this passage, it is possible to imagine Lefebvre at his window and gather a sense of him listening and looking into the street. While the chaos of noise alone 'has no rhythm', 'the attentive ear begins to separate out, to distinguish the sources, to bring them back together to perceive interactions' (2004: 27). Earlier, Lefebvre has instructed that the rhythmanalyst 'will listen to the world, and above all to what are disdainfully called noises, which are said without meaning, and to *murmurs* [rumeurs], full of meaning – and finally he will listen to silences' (19). In the first instance then, the body

---

[15] Lefebvre's language is not gender-neutral. I don't draw attention to this in later quotes.

is the central tool to apprehend rhythm. Indeed: 'The theory of rhythms is founded on the experience and knowledge [*connaissance*] of the body' (67). The body 'consists of a bundle of rhythms, different but in tune', a polyrhythmic and eurhythmic ensemble. The rhythmanalyst 'listens – and first to his body; he learns rhythm from it, in order consequently to appreciate external rhythms'. The rhythmanalyst attends to the entirety of a situation in an integrated way 'taking his own rhythms as a reference' such that the body serves as a 'metronome' in relation to broader patterns and interactions (19–20).

So to practice rhythmanalysis, we feel new rhythms in relation to existing ones, related to the heart beating, breathing or normal patterns of work, rest, waking and sleep. For Lefebvre, 'Rhythms always need a reference: the initial moment persists through other perceived givens' (2004: 36) which informs how we describe them, as plodding, lively, intense and so on. However, Lefebvre also recognizes rhythm as having a calculable 'speed, frequency [and] consistency' which make up the measure of each rhythm (10). Although he emphasizes rhythmanalysis as embodied, he does not disregard methods which document some aspects of rhythm quantitatively (DeLyser and Sui 2012).

For the most part, Lefebvre focuses on rhythmanalysis as immersive, requiring phenomenological tools: 'The rhythmanalyst calls on all his senses. ... He thinks with his body, not in the abstract, but in lived temporality' (Lefebvre 2004: 21). Indeed, 'to grasp a rhythm, it is necessary to have been **grasped** by it; one must let oneself go, give oneself over, abandon oneself to its duration' (27, emphasis in original). This implies 'the cultivation of a peculiar style of attentiveness' to become susceptible to rhythm (McCormack 2013: 42, 50) as 'the effort to discern and note this one [rhythm] or that one imposes itself perpetually' (Lefebvre 2004: 21). While Lefebvre talks about the body and all the senses, he highlights the aural: 'The discriminatory capacity of the auditory and cerebral apparatus plays the primary role – practical and spontaneous – in the grasping of rhythm' (Lefebvre 2004: 69).

If the rhythmanalyst 'must simultaneously catch a rhythm and perceive it within the whole' and 'arrive at the **concrete** through experience' (2004: 21, emphasis in original), this may be insufficient. 'In order to grasp and analyse rhythms, it is necessary to get outside them, but not completely,' Lefebvre writes, since rhythm is at the same time linked to 'logical categories and mathematical calculations' and to 'the visceral and vital body' (17, 14). We therefore need 'critical distance' (Elden 2004a: 113) as well as immersion to do rhythmanalysis. Rhythmanalysis is both a 'practico-sensory and intellectual' practice, corporeal and conceptual (McCormack 2013: 42).

Second, if rhythmanalysis is 'a sort of meditation on time, the city, people' (Lefebvre 2004: 30), timing, in the sense of both scheduling and duration, matters for the perception of rhythm. Lefebvre provides an instance of the imperceptibility of rhythm within certain viewpoints and time frames: 'Overlooking the gardens, the differences between habitual (daily, therefore linked to night and day) rhythms blur; they seem to disappear into a structural immobility.' We cannot get beyond the apparent stillness of the scene. It is light that literally makes the difference here, sun and shadows. And the form of attention which the rhythmanalyst brings to bear on the setting: 'Look harder and longer,' Lefebvre entreats us, 'go deeper ... listen attentively instead of simply looking.' 'Continue and you will see this garden and the *objects* ... **polyrhythmically**, or if you prefer *symphonically*', each 'having its own time above the whole' (30, emphases in original). After all, there is 'nothing inert in the *world*' just 'the apparent immobility [of the garden] that contains one thousand and one movements' (17). The *release* of rhythms 'demands attention and a certain time' (32).

Third, positioning in space is crucial. In terms of doing rhythmanalysis, if we accept that the body is central, where should the rhythmanalyst locate his or her body in time and space? When trying to grasp the rhythm of the street, 'a balcony does the job admirably', asserts Lefebvre, allowing the rhythmanalyst to achieve an inside–outside ideal – to 'situate oneself simultaneously inside and outside' – as in the spirit of ethnography more generally. Failing access to this 'marvellous invention', a window will have to do he says so long as the view is appropriate. In contrast to the immersion of the street, the balcony/window permits the disentangling of the flow of sounds and movements and the clarity of interaction the rhythmanalyst seeks to identify. From here, he notices how 'people produce completely different noises when the cars stop: feet and words'; there's 'a second of silence and then it's the rush'. And, using a metaphor from nature, how when cars stall in the road, 'pedestrians move around them like waves around a rock'. Colour and density are also important for reading the scene: 'Amongst the flurry of cars, pedestrians cluster together, a clot here, a lump over there; grey dominates, with multicoloured flecks, and these heaps break apart for the race ahead' (2004: 27–9).

If 'being there' is important for undertaking rhythmanalysis, Lefebvre also recognizes the absent presence of what we do not directly encounter, what in effect lies beyond the 'sensible and visible order'. The State is not seen from the window he remarks, but it 'looms over this present, this omnipresent State' (2004: 32) – and, he argues, is incidentally doing the work of capital. In an earlier passage, he explicitly asks: 'Might there be hidden, **secret**, rhythms hence inaccessible movements and temporalities?' 'No' he replies. For him secret rhythms are only rhythms that are obscured (in physiology or settled in memory but unspoken) but they are not unknown (2004: 17–18, emphasis in original). Lefebvre contends that different presents are alive in 'the present', for instance, on economo-political society, he comments: 'The visible moving parts hide the machinery' (15). The challenge is to uncover it.

In the instance of rhythmanalysis from the window discussed above, the body is immobile in space and the attention of eyes and ears is largely directed outwards, albeit in relation to the body's inner rhythms. However, rhythmanalysis mostly happens on the move and in 'Rhythmanalysis of Mediterranean Cities' originally published with Régulier in 1986, Lefebvre offers a broader account of rhythm from the street. This work takes its starting point from Fernand Braudel and the *Annales* school of historical research which emphasized the longue durée of historical time rather than specific events in social change. Instead of focusing on particluar cities, the Mediterranean large town or city of this essay is therefore considered as one through its shared features of the presence of waves, climate and commercial relations (Lefebvre and Régulier 2004b: 91).

At the outset, this feels at odds with Lefebvre's detailed attention to the body and the deployment of the senses in social space. It is not clear in this essay when or where Lefebvre – or Régulier – is located in time or place and how or in relation to which rhythmic elements of the everyday they deploy their bodies and senses. It's slightly disappointing after the earlier excitement of what rhythmanalysis might offer. That said, there are wonderful segments which evoke the intertwining of time and space, architecture and movement. The discussion of the role of steps and stairs in Mediterranean architecture in particular in Venice and at the Gare de Saint Charles in Marseille exposes the time spaces of the built environment:[16] 'a link between spaces, the stairway also ensures a link between times'. The authors spell out what this means for people to move around urban space.

---

[16] See Stanek (2011) for a discussion of Lefebvre's thinking on architecture.

Steps 'rhythm the walk through the city' in Venice; and in Marseille, 'their screaming monumentality imposes on the body and on consciousness the requirement of passing from one rhythm to another, as yet unknown – to be discovered' (2004b: 97).

Rhythmanalysis: A provisional assessment

Having closely reviewed Lefebvre's concepts and practices of rhythmanalysis, where does this leave a present-day researcher preparing to do rhythmanalysis? This section briefly considers some critiques of Lefebvre before the next part of the chapter shows how researchers have subsequently worked with rhythmanalysis across different fields.

Scholars broadly agree that Lefebvre offers a useful conceptual repertoire of rhythm and some indications for doing rhythmanalysis. These are important and valuable contributions to the social sciences, if not to the extent that Lefebvre claimed in his remarks on founding 'a new science'. There are other reservations. First, Simpson (2008) critiques Lefebvre's elision of linear time with the temporality of capitalism, pointing out that this leaves little room for other practices and perspectives. In his own research he shows how street performers in Covent Garden in London play with different rhythms, mobilizing them in their performances with more fluidity than Lefebvre suggests is possible. Furthermore, although rhythmanalysis is interested in jarring in the everyday for its potential to generate creative differences – or moments – McCormack argues that Lefebvre nevertheless pathologizes arrhythmia (2013: 52–3). Blue also nuances the relations between some of Lefebvre's concepts: eurhythmia and arrhythmia are not to be understood in opposition to one another, he argues since eurhythmia 'already contains arrhythmia, pauses, breaks and off-beats' (2017: 20).

Second, the body of Lefebvre's rhythmanalyst is an ambiguous one on the threshold between social and biological, public and private. According to Merrifield (who is rather dismissive of *Rhythmanalysis*) the book was a provocation against those 'who document only what they see and not what they feel or hear' (2006: 75). In *Rhythmanalysis* and more generally Lefebvre's methodology is a form of 'participant observation' (Merrifield 2006: 4) but one that is corporeally and sensorially attuned (Potts 2015: 550). For Lefebvre, *Rhythmanalysis* never loses sight of the body (2004: 67).

However, Simpson argues that the body Lefebvre presents is 'acted upon' (2008: 233) or in the words of Borch, Bondo Hansen and Lange, it is 'an effect of society' (2015: 1083). Furthermore, Burgin argues that Lefebvre has a 'passive understanding of perception' which might lead him to miss the 'creative dynamics of rhythm' (1996 in Revill 2013: 58). In contrast, Simonsen contends that Lefebvre transcends the division between the active body and the body that is acted upon although she points out that 'a tension between biological and social processes remains unsolved' and calls for a more attuned understanding of the body in relation to gender and sexuality (2005: 9–10).

Famously for Lefebvre, it is bodies which produce or generate space as they move such that bodies and spaces are not discrete. Bodies themselves are understood as 'spacetimes generated though the constructive entrainment and interference of a multiplicity of rhythms' (McCormack 2013: 42) – 'traversed by rhythms as the "ether" is traversed by waves', as Lefebvre puts it (1991: 206). Lefebvre is very clear about the capacities of his own body but also surprisingly firm in his refusal to deepen his understanding of his own body through rhythmanalysis: 'For reasons I am unaware of, I have always preserved a very strong sense of my own body. ... My body knows what it wants, what it needs. ... It is to my fortunate bodily make-up that I owe my unshakable health and vitality' (2014b: 34–5).

Working with rhythmanalysis

The idea of rhythmanalysis has intrigued a growing number of scholars in recent years and there is now a significant body of work which has taken it in different directions in fields from health and education to cultural theory and sound art. Geographers figure prominently in its recent history. From a position which privileged space and spatial relations, geographers have been attuned to relationships between space and time. In contrast, while historians, sociologists and other social scientists have long been attentive to temporality, only recently have they come to recognize space as constitutive of the social rather than as a backdrop to social relations. But the internal dynamics of disciplines is only part of the story here. The appeal of rhythmanalysis as a way of researching space and time together in the twenty-first century is for how it chimes with the way that the world seems to be changing. Lefebvre's cyclical and linear rhythms are relevant

36 What is rhythmanalysis?

for making sense of the fragmented routines of fast-food service workers on zero hours contracts, the challenges of childcare and its synchronization with other commitments, and the pace and pressures of academic life. Rhythm is relevant beyond the patterns of everyday lives too at the scale of broader social change. 'There is a case', write Henriques, Tianen and Väliaho, 'to think about rhythm as a pervasive force and a critical concept when it comes to mapping larger socio-political developments in [and perhaps beyond] modernity' (2014: 14).

In this part of the chapter I have selected areas where empirical research using rhythmanalysis has been strongest: cultural and historical rhythmanalysis; rhythm and mobility; the rhythms of place and place-making; working rhythms; and the rhythms of nature. This selection leaves aside other contributions, for instance rhythmanalyses of television (Obert 2008), sleep (Meadows, Nettleton and Neale 2017), identity (Edensor 2006; O'Connor 2017), digital spaces (Davies 2018), institutional practices (Blue 2017; Southerton 2013; Mylan and Southerton 2017) relations to the non-human (Evans and Franklin 2010) and the life-course (Stratford 2015). I would just make readers aware of two recent books which open other fields to rhythmanalysis. Michael Alhadeff-Jones' *Time and the Rhythms of Emancipatory Education* (2017) explores rhythm as formation, reconsidering the way time might be envisaged in and beyond education and Tom Apperley's *Gaming Rhythms* (2010) uses rhythmanalysis to examine the interconnected rhythms of digital game play that cut across local and global scales.

Cultural historical rhythmanalysis

In an instance of cultural historical rhythmanalysis, Ben Highmore (2002) offers a rhythmanalytical reading of photographs from Thomson and Smith's *Street Life in London* published from February 1877 to January 1878. He explores the 'politics of pace' he identifies in Lefebvre's work in these images to release 'captured rhythms' and different tempos of social life, teasing out 'something of the actuality of urban life' that remains in them (176–7). Yi Chen's book *Practising Rhythmanalysis* is also an important engagement with rhythmanalysis as an instance of cultural historical analysis. Her subject is the 'orchestrated rhythmic relationships' and 'temporal-spatial entanglements' of the British postal system in the 1970s as a moment of rhythmic disruption and broader political change. This was a time of the decline of the social practice of writing and sending letters, and the rise of

Direct Mail and home shopping. She traces rhythm as the *'effects'* of time space practices in the discourses of archived materials (2017: 61, emphasis in original).

Rhythm and mobility

Lefebvre warned: 'We easily confuse *rhythm* with *movement*' (2004: 5, emphasis in original). He suggests that a sequence of movements alone do not necessarily produce rhythm. It may be that recent interest in the field of mobilities (Urry 2007) and the sociology of speed (Wacjman and Dodd 2017) have sidelined the recognition of rhythm. Indeed, Edensor (2011) has argued that there has been limited attention to the relation between mobility and temporality (although his own work makes an important contribution here, see Chapter 3). In this section, I highlight research which explores rhythm on the move.

There has been a surge of interest in walking in the social sciences in recent years, both as a subject of study and as a method of conducting research (Ingold and Vergunst 2008; Middleton 2009, 2010; Pierce and Lawhon 2015; Wunderlich 2008, 2010, 2013), for instance in mobile interviews (Clark and Emmel 2010; Evans and Jones 2011) and 'go-along' ethnography (Kusenbach 2003; Pink et al. 2010). Recognized as a 'muscular consciousness' (Bachelard 1964: 11 in Chen 2013: 531) and a means of 'creating new embodied ways of knowing' (Pink et al. 2010: 1), walking has recently been developed as a multi-sensory research practice.[17] This involves observation and interaction according to the 'places and paces' of participants' lives which enable 'an understanding of the social world evermore congruent with people's lived experiences of it' (Bates and Rhys-Taylor 2017). With a particular focus on rhythm, Jennie Middleton (2009, 2010) analyses the multiple forms of rhythm, temporality and spatiality that walking encompasses. Through interviews and diary entries (including photographs) she considers people's awareness of 'experiential time' and the embodied, technological and material practices and relations of walking. Similarly, Filipa Wunderlich (2008, 2010, 2013) undertakes detailed studies of the rhythms of walking through attention to small movements in specific places across short stretches of time. She highlights walking as haptic – feet touching the ground alongside other bodily connections

---

[17] See, for example, WalkingLab projects: https://walkinglab.org/

to the environment. She argues that this gives rise to different place-temporalities and place-rhythms.

If walking has had a notable appeal for mobilities scholars, studies of rhythm and mobility also include running (Edensor, Kärrholm and Wirdelöv 2017; Edensor and Larsen 2017), cycling (Cook and Edensor 2017; Spinney 2010), commuting (Edensor 2011), steamship rhythms (Anim-Addo 2014), rail travel (Revill 2013), coach travel (Edensor and Holloway 2008) and ferry travel (Vannini 2012a) as well as the relations of movement and stillness (Bissell and Fuller 2011). I briefly discuss two examples of ferry travel and children's school journeys which highlight the use of rhythmanalysis in some interesting ways.

Rhythmanalysis has the capacity to make visible the relationship between individual and social rhythms. We see this in the constellations of rhythms of the various 'rush hours' in towns and cities across the world. Philip Vannini's (2012a) account of everyday ferry travel in the watery world of Canada's west coast and islands is particularly powerful in juxtaposing individual and social rhythms as ferry-users move 'in' and 'out of time' between urban space and the slower modes of island life. He uses rhythmanalysis to attend to the pace of life of the places the ferries serve as connecting 'lifelines' (243). However, he argues that rhythm needs to be supplemented by both *speed* and *duration* to better understand temporality and mobility (245) although I would suggest that speed and duration might equally be read as properties of rhythm.

Kim Kullman and Charlotte Palludan's (2011) study of children's mobility in Denmark and Finland shows how rhythmanalysis can be used – following Elden (2004b) – as a *tool* of analysis, not just an object of attention, and one that has implications for education and social policy as well as urban planning. The authors demonstrate how children's everyday life takes place across different rhythmic registers and they stress the diversity of the embodied routines children learn on their journeys to and from school. This refines Lefebvre's emphasis on spatial and corporeal regulation through dressage as children are seen to 'shift flexibly between different rhythms, varying them as they go along' (354). The notion of 'dancing' with its emphasis on improvisation within or alongside choreographed sequences might better describe children's mobile agencies than Lefebvre's dressage alone, they argue, pointing out resonances with Nigel Thrift's (2007) emphasis on dancing to capture how people skilfully navigate the city.

The rhythms of place and place-making

'The interaction of diverse, repetitive and different rhythms animates, as one says, the street and the neighbourhood,' Lefebvre writes (2004: 30). Rhythm shapes a mobile sense or experience of place, and places might be characterized by the 'ensemble of rhythms' that permeate them (Edensor 2010b: 69). Rhythmanalysts conceive of place as arising from the intersection of multiple mobile rhythms in the built environment which means that studies of mobility often contribute to an understanding of place and place-making. Rhythmanalysis shows how places are made: through mobile flows of capital, people, objects, energy or matter 'which course through and around them'. It 'emphasizes the dynamic and processual qualities of place' identifying the 'rhythms through which spatial order is sustained'. Places then are sites in which multiple temporalities come together, in harmony or at odds with one another to produce an 'ever changing polyrhythmic constellation' (Edensor 2011: 190–1), and less chaos than might be expected as rhythm orders time and space (Amin and Thrift 2002).

Rhythmanalysis has been widely used to study place, especially city space including in historical accounts of urban street life (e.g. Highmore 2002 as discussed earlier), everyday routines in contemporary urban spaces (Chen 2013; Degen 2010; Hall 2010; Smith and Hall 2013; Sgibnev 2015), gentrification (Degen 2008; Kern 2016), gender and ethnic inequalities in the night-time economy (Schwanen et al. 2012), absence (Gibas 2013), consumption (Cronin 2006; Kärrholm 2009), street performance (Simpson 2008, 2012), festival spaces (Duffy et al. 2011), domestic space (Nansen et al. 2009), imagined space (Weizman 2000), the sounds (Bull 2000; Labelle 2008, 2010) and senses (Degen 2008) of the city. In their introduction to a special issue of *The Sociological Review* on 'Urban Rhythms', Rob Smith and Kevin Hetherington argue that 'a critical consideration of rhythm allows for an understanding of the contemporary urban era that distinguishes it from those of the past' (2013: 5). In other words, different times and places are characterized by different rhythms. Below, I discuss two examples of place-rhythms to highlight different possibilities of rhythmanalysis.

First, rhythmanalysis can uncover the sensory city as in Monica Degen's *Sensing Cities* (2008), a comparative sensory ethnography of gentrification in Manchester and Barcelona. Lefebvre informs Degen's research design and her attention to urban space is constituted through 'the sensory-practico body'. She makes a distinction between 'activity rhythms' which refer to daily movements and repetitive spatial practices and 'sensory rhythms' through which 'the senses map a particular landscape' (51). In the practice of rhythmanalysis, she develops what she calls sensory maps of different areas based on the descriptions her interviewees offer. These allow her to characterize places beyond her own and any one of her interviewees' senses of them, for instance as a 'spectacular' or 'dwelling' space (174–5).

Second, sound is an important counter to the dominance of the visual in accounts of urban experience. Michael Bull's (2000) ethnography of the use of personal stereos in urban space contributes to an auditory understanding of the self in/and of the city. Personal stereo users listening to music sidestep the imposition of linear rhythms as they carve out 'segments' of time on the move with autonomy and privacy or 'concentrate on mood maintenance that overcomes the journey time' itself. Rhythmic moments emerge through repeated listening to the same song and time is reclaimed as the cyclical reasserts itself, temporarily at least. In Brandon LaBelle's (2008, 2010) work, sound and music are further explored as a means of ordering the self within urban environments. As rhythm is embodied and experienced in sound, so in turn music and sound shape the rhythms of the city.

Working rhythms

Rhythm has long informed norms, practices and understandings of work. The development of clock-time as a form of work-discipline in the industrial revolution parcelled the day and night into linear stretches of work and non-work time and set the pace for both (Thompson 1967). Time and motion studies were a further means of the regulation of workers' bodies in the name of efficiency in the early twentieth century (discussed in Chapter 1). Recent attention has focused on the loss of rhythm and skill in craft-based working (Ocejo 2017; Sennett 2009), the effects of industrialization on the body and voice of workers (Korczynski, Pickering and Robertson 2013; Korczynski 2014; Wolkowitz 2006), and the recognition of new temporal demands and modes of time-discipline imposed on the working body under flexible capitalism in the twenty-first century (Sharma 2014; Snyder 2016). Lefebvre's rhythmanalysis has much to offer this field and in recent years it has been explicitly used to study work, including the performance of work (Simpson 2008, 2012; Snyder 2016), the procrastinating body's refusal of work (Potts 2010), the rhythmic ordering of organizational life and the socio-economic relations of work (Borch, Bondo Hansen and Lange 2015; Lyon 2016).

An appeal to rhythm for different ways of living and working is important in studies which explore alternatives to the dominant pace and shape of capitalism (Crawford 2010; Dey at al. 2016; Pettinger 2017; Vannini and Taggart 2014). Below, two examples highlight the usefulness of Lefebvre's concepts and approach for this field in different ways. (Borch, Bondo Hansen and Lange 2015 and Lyon 2016 are discussed in depth in Chapter 3 so do not feature here.)

Ben Snyder's book *The Disrupted Workplace* is about work, time and rhythm under flexible capitalism and is based on ethnographies conducted in the United States of the temporal trends and pressures in the working practices of financial professionals, long-distance lorry drivers and job seekers. Among the financial traders Snyder interviews and observes, 'dealmakers' must be constantly available, always 'on' leading to 'chronic desynchronization from the normative clock and calendar rhythms' (2016: 58). In a striking account of especially intense deal-making, one trader, Chuck, tells Snyder of the tensions that accrue in his neck and back and how 'I'll wrap my legs around the legs of my chair' when his mind is running at 'hyper-speed' but his body is still, eyes fixed to his screen (80–1). Chuck as well as Snyder are both rhythmanalysts here.

The site of Phil Jones and Saskia Warren's research (2016) is the so-called creative sector in which hopes of post-industrial economic success are often invested. The authors draw parallels between Sarah Sharma's (2014) notion of 'recalibration' and Lefebvre's concept of dressage. For Sharma, bodies must be realigned – or recalibrated – according to the times that serve the needs of capital (Jones and Warren 2016: 287). These new relations to time – and space – have come to be experienced and performed as normal in what Freeman (2010) calls *chrononormativity*. In the creative and cultural sector, however, it is rhythm rather than clock-time per se which 'is the key mechanism regulating the lives of its workers' (Jones and Warren 2016: 289). The approach and methods Jones and Warren use make it possible to reach this insight. They collected data from conventional and video interviews, activity diaries and focus groups, with a focus on the '*felt* experience of time' (289, emphasis in original) rather than time as quantity in which the details of the hours risk obscuring the rhythms of work. Patterns of work in the sector were shown to be at odds with the recognized intrinsic rhythms of creative production in an instance of profound arrhythmic disjuncture. In these cases, rhythmanalysis offers a critique of alienation and the possibility of imagining different rhythms of work.

Image 2.2 Tides, Isle of Sheppey, UK, 28 May 2017 (Author's own images).

The rhythms of nature

Lefebvre was clear, as we heard earlier, that when looking into the garden from his apartment, the rhythms of nature as well as the rhythms of the city could be equally apprehended through rhythmanalysis. Several scholars have explicitly used rhythmanalysis to study the natural world. Owain Jones has explored the natural rhythms of the tides (Jones 2011) and in collaboration with Michaela Palmer (Palmer and Jones 2014) has produced fascinating 'sonifications' of tidal and other non-human patterns that are not directly accessible to human senses. While we can see tides as they break on the shore and hear the movement of the waves directly (see Image 2.2), we cannot grasp the rhythms that lie under the surface of the water and move it in and out of an estuary or around the coast for instance, along with silt and other suspended elements. Palmer and Jones' sonifications make it possible to access these rhythms and so transcend the limits of bodily perception.[18]

Two further examples draw attention to different situations where the human world is subject to an unanticipated natural event: a snowstorm and an earthquake. Julia Bennett (2015) explores 'ontological belonging' as a rhythmic practice achieved through habit, repetition and synchronization. Her research is based on diaries which she contends are more effective than (researcher) observation as they can be completed on the participants' own terms – and rhythms – in their private spaces. They thereby offer the 'present-but-outside perspective that rhythmanalysis requires' (960–1). She discusses the diary of a research participant written over the course of a week when 'snowed in'. In John's accounts, mundane rhythms are made clear by the disruption of the weather; at the same time his diary reveals the collective 'off beats' that are created in these out-of-the-ordinary circumstances. In a more profound instance of arrhythmia, the Christchurch earthquake which shook New Zealand in February 2011 is the subject of Holly Thorpe's (2015) rhythmanalysis. She explores the impact on the bodies and mobilities of those affected, especially in relation to their sporting routines which took place in or around the city such as skateboarding, surfing, biking and climbing. Residents found creative ways of sustaining sport in the aftermath of the earthquake and these were a powerful tonic for reasserting familiar rhythms and connections to place as well as for forming a post-disaster spatial imaginary.

---

[18] I discuss sonifications further in the final part of Chapter 4.

Conclusions

This chapter has provided an overview of the ways in which rhythmanalysis has been conceptualized, practised and developed by Lefebvre and others. It has shown how rhythmanalysis can be employed as a research strategy to reveal the workings of rhythm across a wide variety of fields. This requires methods that are sensitive to detecting rhythm and these will necessarily vary by context. Chapter 3 now considers three sets of examples in more depth to highlight differences in the formulation of rhythmanalysis and the range of techniques they imply.

3 Key methodological orientations in doing rhythmanalysis: The body as central, displaced or insufficient

Introduction

Chapter 2 considered how Lefebvre himself envisaged and undertook rhythmanalysis. It then provided an overview of how rhythmanalysis has been taken up and developed in recent research across the social sciences. This chapter goes into more depth on the methodological strategies and practices used by contemporary researchers of rhythm. I have chosen to focus here on three examples which operationalize rhythmanalysis as an embodied research practice in three different ways: where the body is central, displaced or insufficient.

The first example is actually a series of rhythmanalytical projects undertaken by the British cultural geographer Tim Edensor. Here, the body is *central* to doing rhythmanalysis and is deployed as a key tool in the research process. In this approach, the body is an autoethnographic and metronomic device for registering rhythm at a corporeal scale, for sensing rhythm in the practices and performances of others through empathy and imagination, and for analysing other people's narrative accounts of embodied rhythms.

In contrast, in the second example the body is present but *displaced* as it cannot directly register rhythm. Researchers at Copenhagen Business School, Christian Borch, Kristian Bondo Hansen and Ann-Christina Lange, analyse the work of high-frequency traders in financial markets whose bodies are calibrated to their algorithms rather than to one another as was the case in a more traditional and immersive 'pit' market. This example demonstrates rhythmanalysis as a material method and as one which analyses 'how *capital's own everyday* is organized' (Borch, Bondo Hansen and Lange 2015: 1082, emphasis in original). In it the body is still present as a tool of research but is no longer central.

From finance to fish, the third example is from my own research where the body is necessary but *insufficient* to record the rhythms of the market (Lyon 2016). It focuses on the use of audiovisual methods and the construction of an audiovisual montage based on time-lapse photography and sound recordings as a means to identify different coexisting rhythms in the fish market.

Example one: The centrality of the body in research on rhythm and mobility

As discussed in Chapter 2, Lefebvre calls for the rhythmanalyst to use his or her own body as a central device or research tool for revealing rhythm: 'To grasp a rhythm, it is necessary to have been *grasped* by it; one must let oneself go, give oneself over, abandon oneself to its duration.' It is equally important to retain the capacity to shake off that rhythm, to perceive it critically as if from the 'outside' (2004: 27, emphasis in original). In this section, I discuss research which does just that: the rhythmanalytical geography of Tim Edensor. *Geographies of Rhythm*, edited by Edensor and published in 2010, did much to advance discussion of rhythm within and beyond geography, demonstrating the gain of developing Lefebvre's thinking to understand the multiple temporalities of everyday life in the twenty-first century, from 'ravalejar' (an invented verb conjuring a way of living in El Raval, Barcelona) to rumba. Edensor (and colleagues) has undertaken multiple studies of rhythm, most related to place-making and mobility, including walking, running, cycling, driving and dancing. The following discussion draws out the gain of 'grasping' rhythm with the body for advancing understanding, and it critically considers the different combinations of techniques Edensor employs for apprehending rhythm.

Walking in rhythm

Let's start with walking. The activity of walking has long been documented as an embodied routine of everyday life (de Certeau 1984; Solnit 2014) and is widely used in arts practice.[1] Edensor (2000, 2008, 2010b) shows

---

[1] Most famously perhaps in the Anglophone art world in Richard Long's work: http://www.richardlong.org

how the production of place happens (in part) through the collective choreographies of walking. The cross-cutting movements of people give rise to an 'ensemble of rhythms' and a 'complex polyrhythmy of place' through which 'time and space are stitched together' (Edensor 2010b: 77, 70). The rhythmic qualities of walking, whether smooth and 'eurhythmic' or uneven and 'arrhythmic', intersect with one another to produce place collectively. The extent to which they are coordinated and synchronized by institutional arrangements is evident as people's paths converge at workplaces, shops, cafes and parks then separate out again as they continue on their way.

This does not happen spontaneously. Edensor makes use of Lefebvre's concept of dressage to recognize the regulation of embodied rhythms, and how the supposedly natural practice of walking is 'styled' by socio-economic and cultural norms in specific times and places. Dressage underlies how pedestrians accommodate other moving objects – people, bicycles, cars – or comply with the ways their mobility is channelled – in museum visits for instance, or more strikingly in the regulation of public space which refuses the stationary bodies of the homeless (Blomley 2007). At the same time, these normative rhythms do not wholly compel or control: 'Whatever regime of spatial ordering persists, the body can never be assumed to passively acquiesce in the performance of a dance of duty' (Edensor 2000: 137). Walking is therefore both regulated *and* escapes that regulation.

This tension is clear in Edensor's (2010b) reflections (with Lefebvre) on the mobile interventions of several artists. First, Richard Long emphasizes the emergent and novel properties of walking; in other words, how 'difference' in Lefebvre's terms is inherent in and produced by repetition (as discussed in Chapter 2). Through walking we become aware of pace and speed, and tune into different relationships, forces, sounds and atmospheres. Second, Francis Alys causes an arrhythmic stir in *Railings* where he drags a stick along metal barriers in central London. This creates a new rhythmic experience of moving through city space that is both repetitive and disjunctive and which gives rise to an awareness of 'architectural features and material qualities' and the privatization of space in the capital. Edensor points out how Alys extends thinking and performing the walking body 'beyond the feet', embracing rhythmanalysis in a more fully sensual register. A third example is Jeremy Deller's *Procession* in central Manchester in 2009 where the absence of dressage which characterizes more formal parades makes way for greater improvisational and expressive modes. While these examples are at some remove from the everyday experience of walking in cities, they bring to the fore the presence and operation of rhythm and the disciplining of bodies in urban space and thereby offer useful tactics for the rhythmanalyst.

In an earlier project, Edensor undertook walking as a form of autoethnography. In a bazaar area of the north Indian city of Agra, he documented how 'the walking body must continuously adapt to the contingencies, flows, materialities and interruptions' of the street (Edensor 2000, 2010b: 73). The bazaar is a porous space used at any one time in multiple ways. It awakens the senses of the stranger as she or he becomes aware of what bodies (human and non-human) do in space and what the space does to them. Edensor highlights the 'improvisational' quality of walking for how it pushes walker-rhythmanalysts to recognize themselves as subjects who must employ active thinking – how to navigate various obstacles; as steeped in habits and routines – such as the gendered gestures of stepping aside for others or pushing through a crowd; and who move in accordance with familiar embodied practices – knowing the length of one's stride and the power of one's legs for instance. In a similar way, Edensor's walks through ruins (2008) emphasize improvisation as the walker encounters irregular physical and material surfaces and textures in these disorderly spaces. The body is enlivened as a path 'evolves' and the walker develops 'a staccato rhythm rather than a repetitive pulse' (2008: 127). The body makes itself felt through 'hunger, blisters, [and] sore muscles' (Edensor 2010b: 73). Through this combination of liveliness and disruption around the body or underfoot, it is possible to see how we might quite literally use our bodies to tune into the multitude of competing rhythms that permeate places. The act of walking attentively is both a first step in sensitizing the body to rhythm and offers an explicit strategy for doing rhythmanalysis (see also Wunderlich 2008, 2013, discussed in Chapter 4).

Edensor is critical of abstract discussions of the body that tend to 'eclipse the lived bodily experience of city life' or accounts that put forward a 'disembodied view of what is an intensely somatic experience' (2000: 121, 130). He also refuses the use of narrative alone to 'talk the walk' as the material experience of walking through a ruin 'is not usually amenable to authoritative representation', he argues (2008: 123). Indeed, his writing on ruins is interspersed with evocative black and white images of the site. However, what is curiously absent from both his account of the bazaar and the ruin is any sense of the fleshy materiality of his own body in place. The reader learns little about his gender and ethnicity – beyond his name – and get no more than a glimpse of his class background when he reveals that walking in ruins stirs memories of factory work, his own and that of 'long-dead working class relatives' (2008: 137). There is talk of materiality and muscles in a general sense but not what the walk felt like to him. This feels like a missed opportunity. A more explicit and reflexive use the rhythmanalyst's own body might foreground the operation of power through rhythm, for instance to expose the 'gendered conventions' (2000: 134) (among others) that he refers to as being present in the life of the bazaar.

On the move by coach and car

Picking up the pace, I now consider mobility and rhythm in two forms of vehicular travel: the commuter's car and the coach tour. First, with a focus on the 'experiential dimensions of commuting rhythms', Edensor draws out the 'pleasures and frustrations' of commuting. If rhythms are 'difficult to knowingly contravene', mobile subjects are not necessarily 'subservient' to traffic flow and find ways to 'appropriate time'. Gemma, a young woman who travels the twenty-three miles between Crewe and Macclesfield in the north of England for work, is the focus of this study. Gemma settles on her cross-country route according to the whim and mood of the day. There are variations in her journey time from forty-five minutes to one and a half hours which she experiences as 'an eternity' at times and as a 'flash' at others. Against the dominant representations of commuting as stultifying, 'a dystopian alienating practice', the extracts from Gemma's account reveal her lively and enlivened state of being on the road and on the move 'drinking in the feeling it gives you' (2011: 189, 192–4, 196, 199–200).

Although she is by herself in the car, Gemma nevertheless experiences her journey as shared: 'I am not alone,' she declares. Indeed, when she spots one of her '"drive by" people' (i.e. other drivers she regularly sees on the road) in a different context, she finds herself saying 'hello' despite the person not recognizing her. This attachment shows the depth to which she senses her journey as synchronized with others despite it remaining a secluded experience. She also appreciates the 'rhythmic predictability' of the stretches of solitary time she has in the car and the opportunity to be expressive: 'To shout, scream, cry, laugh, sing at the top of my voice and be free with only my self to worry about'. (Edensor 2011: 198). Not all commuting is this free or comfortable of course but this example does show how commuting produces a mobile sense of place and makes it possible for the social and affective dimensions of rhythm to come to the fore.

Second, in their rhythmanalysis of coach travel, Tim Edensor and Julian Holloway discuss the 'rhythmic qualities' of the coach tour as an 'experience of both mobility and situatedness' (2008: 498). Their research is set in the West of Ireland and explores 'the ordering of different rhythmic assemblages'. The tour itself contributes to and reinforces 'the selling of Ireland' and Irishness especially in relation to nature, landscape, and traditions of work and leisure. Tour participants largely see what they expect to see and behave in accordance with the rhythmic norms of their tourist roles – photograph the view, buy a souvenir, get back on the coach – their conduct further styled and sanctioned by the commentaries offered. If the tour drivers' narratives are one 'line of force' affecting the mood and meanings of the tour, the landscape itself is another: its visual offerings of bucolic idyll are interspersed with rural poverty, intrusions into the tourist gaze as documented by the authors' photographs. Edensor and Holloway also focus on the rhythmic forces experienced by tour participants at a corporeal level. They take the tour themselves and directly experience how 'rhythms are architectures of narratives, sensations and embodiment' (483, 489, 491, 499). They come to grasp the lack of 'rhythmic unity' of the tour through participating in it on six different occasions in addition to driving behind it on another. There is a clear methodological gain here of repeatedly undertaking a specific experience and this may be useful for other research.

The tour promotes a certain synchronicity of rhythm as passengers are subject to the motion of the coach on the road and the repetition of similar visual scenes such as telegraph poles, gates and fences. Nevertheless, different bodies react differently to its patterning. Indeed, the authors' grasp of rhythm allows them to appreciate how the temporal regularity of the tour is punctuated by stops and visits, and is never completely standardized as participants negotiate with the drivers in relation to their experience of hunger and thirst, restlessness, and the need to move or go to the toilet at different points. The sheer eventfulness of the excursion also contributes to its arrhythmic character and disrupts its apprehension as solely linear (Edensor and Holloway 2008: 497). The journey is marked by uneven movements and sound, and is disturbed by animals, road surfaces and weather.

In both the articles discussed here, the authors use the narrative accounts of drivers and passengers and, in the case of coach travel, their own embodied experiences to access rhythm. While the body remains the primary instrument of research, the bodies which are bearers of rhythm belong to research participants as well as the author-researchers. Further, in the discussion of commuting, the reader sees Gemma's thoughts presented on the page but gains no sense of her relationship to the researchers. And in the case of coach travel, the reader knows little of the lives of these (perhaps inadvertent?) participants in this research – nor of the ethical decisions that bestowed this role on them. It is interesting to reflect on accessing rhythm 'second-hand' in this way as a means of doing rhythmanalysis.

Much qualitative research in the social sciences is dominated by talk and text and the gains and limitations of this reliance have been well rehearsed in recent years (e.g. Back 2007, Pink 2007), especially in the light of new developments in non-representational (Vannini 2015) and affective methodologies (Knudsen and Stage 2015). In Edensor's work, bodies are central to the story but access to bodily experience is through language and dialogue. First, embodied experience must be verbalized and shared with the researchers. There may be a methodological advantage here: To what extent does talking about rhythm – and perhaps finding oneself talking rhythmically – bring it into conscious awareness? Might we come to know it through speaking it in this way? Alternatively: What does language ignore? The recognition of unconscious and more recently pre-cognitive affective modes of being are important for how we conduct research (e.g. Hollway and Jefferson 2013). Which aspects of the experience of rhythm cannot be spoken? In short, what is beyond the reach of rhythmanalysis conducted in this way? Edensor has previously been critical of narrative arguing that it cannot effectively capture impressions, atmospheres, rhythms, sensations and effects in the case of walking (2008: 137). But these accounts on commuting and coach travel are rich and can be seen as a valuable element of the rhythmanalyst's tool-kit if more effective for some experiences of rhythm than others (cf. Ingold 2011).

Second, it is the author-researchers' voices which dominate these accounts without any reflexive discussion of how we got there. In the case of commuting, selections have clearly been made and on coach travel, there is little direct quotation from the driver and passengers. What is the process by which one set of voices gets translated into another? What does this mean for rendering the lived experience of rhythm? What forms of experience might be missed in the process? Finally, how is knowledge shared in the research team across different roles and expertise? These

52   What is rhythmanalysis?

questions are relevant to the knowledge claims made in much qualitative research and I return to them later.

One image taken from the coach window in Edensor and Holloway's discussion of coach travel (Plate 9: Mobility and visual apprehension; reproduced as Image 3.1) is especially evocative of the 'polyrhythmic

Images 3.1 and 3.2 Seen from the coach window, inside and outside, 2007 (Tim Edensor, with kind permission).

ensemble' of the coach tour and the landscape experienced through mobility that combines the inside and outside of the moving vehicle. The curtains framing one side of the window are also reflected in the glass and are rendered alongside the markings on the road and fence posts designating spatial divisions. Into the distance, the gentle curve of the green hill under a bright blue sky situates the tour participants within broader seasonal rhythms, mesmerizing them as the movement of the coach once again blurs the view. The landscape is thereby experienced as 'a space of rhythms and flows', of 'intersecting trajectories and temporalities' (2008: 497–8). In the second image included here (Image 3.2, not published in the original article) we sense the outside space reflected on the coach as it moves through the landscape. These images are indicative of the role the visual might play in showing and suggesting rhythm – and this is discussed in more detail in Example three in this chapter.

Running in the city and cycling in the dark

The liveliest accounts in Edensor's work are those based on autoethnography and 'embodied thick description' (Snyder 2016: 229). In collaboration with Matthew Cook in order to research cycling, Cook rides and keeps an autoethnographic and reflexive cycling diary for one year which both authors analyse (Cook and Edensor 2017). The experience of running the Berlin marathon is the subject of one study of running (Edensor and Larsen 2017), another based on the urbanized running culture of a park in Malmö, Sweden (Edensor, Kärrholm and Wirdelöv 2017). These accounts demonstrate the value of embodied action and autoethnography as modes of doing rhythmanalysis.

If cycling itself is a rhythmic practice, cycling on a murky night reveals 'the entanglement of sound and touch with the experience of looking'. This sensory mix enhances the presence of rhythm and of the landscape. Cook's thirty years of cycling experience underpins the research design and enables him to perceive the seasonal rhythms of cycling – marked by the routines and schedules of competition and shaped by nature – which are felt in the micro-level rhythms of each ride. To be ready to compete in the spring or summer, 'all the hard work is done in the winter and early spring', Cook writes. After that 'it's too late to change the body'. In addition, the cyclist always confronts 'an emerging landscape' (Cook and Edensor 2017: 12, 2) whether in the textures of the road surface, the liveliness of the natural world, the observation of contrasting forms of transport (road and rail) or the experience of the elements such as wind or rain. For instance, a change in the weather can cause a shift away from a habitual and embodied sense of riding to a conscious awareness of pursuing a particular rhythm in a similar way to the active thinking of the walker discussed above.

The autoethnographic extracts in this article make explicit to both writer and reader the vitality and immediacy of the ride in the dark and the way it stimulates connections and imagination. The cyclist gets glimpses of other lives unfolding at a different pace from his own – 'the smell of wood and coal fires' for instance – and these odours evoke other times, perhaps other 'moments' in Lefebvre's terms. Memory transports the cyclist to his paternal grandparents' house and gives rise to feelings of isolation as he moves through the rural landscape. A further strength of this work is in the recognition of the materiality of the cyclist's rhythm. Cook wears a headlamp (rather than a handlebar lamp) which both 'shapes his gaze' and empowers him to direct it (Cook and Edensor 2017: 15, 7). In addition, the weight of the bike and the coolness of the metal against warm skin are part of the feel of the ride.

Tim Edensor and Jonas Larsen's (2017) analysis of the Berlin marathon weaves two rhythmic processes: running the 'race' itself and the everyday preparation over the previous months and weeks, of both runner and city. In this research, Larsen runs the marathon and captures the movement of his own body with a GoPro camera while Edensor films it as a spectator. Larsen also writes a diary of his preparation and experience of the event and both authors conduct interviews with other runners before and after the race, and cycle and film the length of the route the day after the event. Marathon training – as for the cyclist – contains its own rhythms. To be race-ready implies specific configurations of training in anticipation of the marathon and includes resting as well as running, and developing an understanding of pace and style. The aim is 'to absorb rhythm through prolonged practice so that it becomes habitual' at a corporeal level, as in Lefebvre's dressage (Edensor and Larsen 2017: 7). Preparation also implies material relations around specialized clothing, measurement devices, advice and nutrition. And running routines must accommodate – or be accommodated by – other rhythms and commitments, of work, family or domestic life.

While the rhythmic repetition of marathon training for Larsen is cyclical, it is also situated in linear time directed to the date of the race itself. The days and hours before the race are full of potential arrhythmic obstacles – the demands of travel, friends and family, and the need for rest and focus. Hours ahead of the race, Larsen's account of the micro-temporal arrangements of sleeping, eating and eliminating bodily waste convey the intensity and concentration of this phase. Linear time is important during the race itself as runners strive for a personal best or other record and measure themselves in relation to the clock and Global Positioning System (GPS) data. Unlike the uncertainty which characterizes the unfolding route of the night-time cyclist, the smooth terrain of the marathon track holds few surprises. Nevertheless the runner must focus 'on what is in front of us, and on our watches'. The soundscape is of 'shoes-hitting-the-ground, beeping watches, breathing bodies, sporadic music and almost ever-present clapping and yelling': 'no one says a word'. Training is rewarded as the runners settle into their rhythms and 'synchronise eurhythmically' (Edensor and Larsen 2017: 11–12).

Finally, in a study of the urbanized running culture of a park in Malmö, Sweden, in which Edensor collaborated with Mattias Kärrholm and Johan Wirdelöv (2017), the authors based their analysis on Wirdelöv's running diary kept from spring to autumn 2016 as well as interviews with runners in the park and observations of the intersecting mobilities of the park space. Wirdelöv was not an established runner prior to the research but this unfamiliarity meant he was able to notice much that is strange in 'becoming a runner'. In a similar way to Larsen, he had to absorb rhythm into the body which 'involves on-going negotiations with different rhythms'. First, there was the changing experience of time as Wirdelöv's fitness increased. Second, his body experienced 'a sort of unfolding' as he found new ways of moving through space and developing a smooth rhythm. For some runners this means synchronizing with other runners in 'shared rhythms' – or in relation to other moving objects such as cars or bicycles. Third, his awareness shifted between interior and exterior rhythms as, for instance, he accommodated the faster speed of an approaching runner (4, 7, 12–15).

Across these pieces of research, the methodology of reflexive diary-writing is successful for documenting the rhythms of the run and the ride in and over time. However, given that embodied perception of the world is so central to the practice of rhythmanalysis pursued in these examples, it is important to know something of the bodies that are the instruments of the research, especially since it is well established that different bodies perceive differently. We hear little about Larsen or Wirdelöv. Cook does openly present himself as a fit, middle-aged, white, British male but the linkages between this experience and identity in a general sense and how they may dispose him to apprehend rhythm or in what kinds of rhythms his body is enfolded are not made clear. While the body is certainly present in this research, the analysis offered might be more fully situated in the specific bodies of the researchers. A more explicit autoethnographic orientation might add to the practice of rhythmanalysis here (Adams, Holman Jones and Ellis 2014).

Dancing on the street

The final piece of research I want to discuss in this section concerns dance, one of Lefebvre's 'preferred sphere[s] of experiment' for rhythmanalysis (1991: 205). Here the body is central in a different way from the examples discussed above as the rhythmanalysts explicitly analyse and undertake disruptive performances in urban space. The study I discuss is a collaboration between Tim Edensor and Caitlan Bowdler (Edensor and Bowdler 2015) who use rhythmanalysis to analyse recorded and live site-specific dance performances. The three dance works they discuss[2] in addition to the intervention performed by Bowdler in public space show how 'the quality of moving bodies contributes to the qualities of the spaces in which these bodies move' (McCormack 2008: 1822 in Edensor and Bowdler 2015: 710). Here I focus on *Traffic* (2004), choreographed and performed by Wayne Sables, and the 'experimental geography' (Edensor and Bowdler 2015: 711) undertaken by Bowdler herself.

Sables' *Traffic* is a solo intervention in city space which deliberately disrupts and simultaneously exposes everyday urban rhythms in the flow of pedestrian traffic. It takes place on a Saturday morning on a busy shopping street in Leeds in the north of England. From the publicly available film of the intervention,[3] Sables is seen to position himself in a moving crowd against the current in several ways. First, he is still as the crowd pulses around him. Next, he weaves among pedestrians, cutting in and out, in front and around them. Finally, when he dances more conspicuously, the reach of his movements becomes a new, temporary obstacle in the street and the viewer witnesses how space reshapes itself around him. His

---

[2] Philippe Saire's *Mini-Golf du Petit Chene* (2002), Wayne Sables' *Traffic* (2004), and a piece by the Bristol-based Guerilla Dance Project (2010).

[3] *Traffic* is available on YouTube at: https://www.youtube.com/watch?v=f2B6XXQBpFI&feature=c4-overview-vl&list=PL4ED2CE7C27432A8A

gestures and his stillness both draw the viewer's attention to the regularity and automaticity of the movement of others on the street, especially the 'routines and conventions of walking'. Indeed, in each configuration, Sables 'provides a vivid counterpoint to the collectively steady pace of the pedestrians' as they tread along the pavement which 'confines and channels' them. Dancing bodies 'defamiliarise but also thicken a sense of place'. They alert the onlooker on the street and the rhythmanalyst-viewer of the film to a certain 'consistency to place over time' on the one hand, and to the 'tactics' which might be employed to trouble that steadiness at any moment. Indeed, 'the dancer may act as a sort of rhythmanalyst', explicitly using his or her body as 'an instrument to gauge and identify the rhythms of a place' (Edensor and Bowdler 2015: 710–16).

Using dance as a form of rhythmanalysis is precisely what Caitlan Bowdler sought to do in creating a dance which was also filmed.[4] Performed in Piccadilly Gardens, a park in central Manchester, with a colleague, it was 'embodied and immersive' for the two dancers and an opportunity to trace the reactions of others in the park. The setting is important as the gardens are already a space of play and possibility with fewer restrictions on action and movement than the street. The dancers unsettle the scene in an ambiguous way repeatedly blending their movements into everyday spatial practices such as sitting on a bench, and resurfacing from these poses at odds with the norms of the park as they climb over the same bench for instance. They refuse the pace of others on the bridge and make themselves an obstacle which provokes laughter and uncertainty. This can be seen in the bodies of passers-by who literally do not know where to put themselves. Both of these segments of the film are marked by the passage of birds around or across the dancers, hinting at other non-human rhythms which pervade the same space.

This intervention was an autoethnographic attempt to explore how the dimensions of play, rhythm and habit – previously identified as themes of the videos the authors analyse – are experienced live. This chimes well with Lefebvre: 'Play recalls forgotten depths and summons them up to the light of day. ... Play is a lavish provider of presence and presences' (2014a: 497). Bowdler wrote up her performance experience quickly, seeking to retain the immediacy of the affective and embodied sensations it produced,

---

[4] The film is available on YouTube at: https://www.youtube.com/watch?v=-CiPK-5yUGs&feature=youtu.be

and she viewed the film of it to access otherwise neglected aspects of the performance. It is interesting how she recounts feeling 'as if we were blending into the rhythms of the city' through movement, sound and touch. This might be related to the relative freedom of the park compared to the street of Sables' performance, or that she was one of two dancers moving in coordination with one another. However, it also hints at the varying configurations of rhythms that synchronize across the body and the 'rhythmic diversity' of a place, or in the case of Sables may jar in the face of a hostile reaction. Either way, the sensory grasp of the city is heightened by the 'inventive technique' of the dancer as rhythmanalyst (Edensor and Bowdler 2015: 717, 721, 723).

Reflections

Rhythmanalysis, argues Edensor, is effective for revealing how places are 'seething with emergent properties, but usually stabilized by regular patterns of flow' (2010a: 3). Across his own work he has worked with rhythmanalysis in imaginative and experimental ways and deployed the body as a device to register rhythms, as a source of experience, and as a means to sense rhythm in the actions and performances of others. He has gone beyond the body as a direct medium for grasping rhythm, working with talk, text, and the visual to gain access to rhythm, and has extended the attention of the rhythmanalyst to polyrhythmic ensembles of bodies, materials, atmospheres and environments. It is through this variety of embodied practices that Edensor and collaborators identify different configurations of rhythm. However, if rhythmanalysis is something of a work in progress, it might be further enhanced by more situated accounts of the rhythmanalyst's body, not in the sense of autobiographical revelation for its own sake but to reflexively explore the different levels at which rhythms register for different bodies and what this means for understanding the polyrhythmic complexity of social life.

Example two: The displacement of the body in the study of market rhythms

The second example I have selected to focus on here takes issue with Lefebvre's contention that rhythm is always experienced as embodied. It is based on the insights of Danish researchers, Christian Borch, Kristian Bondo Hansen and Ann-Christina Lange (2015) working in a cross-disciplinary context spanning management, philosophy and politics. This section is shorter than the others in this chapter as it is primarily based on a single study. However, I consider it important for the ways in which it develops rhythmanalysis beyond the body and as a material method.

Borch, Bondo Hansen and Lange argue that existing scholarship using rhythmanalysis to examine everyday life, especially routine urban rhythms, recognizes Lefebvre's concern with the lived experience of capitalism at the level of the everyday. However, there is often 'a lack of systematic empirical attention to how these everyday rhythms are related to *capitalism*' and the connections between mundane practices and the workings of capital may be underspecified or missing altogether. Borch, Bondo Hansen and Lange's study of financial markets as a mid-level space of the operation of capital seeks to address this gap, analysing 'the rhythms of capitalism as expressed in particular configurations of financial markets, rather than how capitalism structures the rhythms of market-external everyday life in the city'. The authors thereby 'relax the strong opposition' that is found in Lefebvre's work between capital on the one hand and everyday life and bodies on the other (2015: 1082, emphasis in original).

Trading in the pit

Borch, Bondo Hansen and Lange (2015) explore the contrasting operation of financial markets from the so-called open-outcry 'pit' of the early twentieth century to current practices of high-frequency trading (HFT). The architecture of the Chicago Board of Trade – their selected example of pit trading – allows everyone on the inside to see and hear one another and has steps to the outside that facilitate the swift processing of orders. A late-nineteenth-century design, it is a 'unified marketplace with maximum visibility' intended to 'enhance market liquidity' and it leads to 'intensive' and 'effective' forms of trade (1087). This intensity is experienced at the level of 'bodily sociality' (MacKenzie 2004: 88 in Borch, Bondo Hansen and Lange 2015: 1087) where traders read one other's physical gestures and signs. In order to tune into the 'language' of the market and its micro-expressions, traders must configure and adjust their minds and bodies to its rhythms (Zaloom 2003 in Borch, Bondo Hansen and Lange 2015: 1087). At the extreme, the trader 'merges' with the market and in so doing gains access to its ebbs and flows. Immersion is the name of the game – or as Borch and colleagues interpret, eurhythmia is the goal. However, this reading of immersion as eurhythmia disregards Lefebvre's arguments that rhythmanalysis always requires critical distance and movement across the inside and the outside (2004: 27). Immersed in the market, the trader feels rhythm but this does not make him or her a rhythmanalyst.

In addition to drawing on existing ethnographic studies, Borch and colleagues make use of an early-twentieth-century fictionalized account of pit trading set in Chicago. *The Pit: A Story of Chicago* published by Frank Norris in 1903 was based on well-known figures and events. Since pit trading was a dominant practice at the time this novel was written, Borch, Bondo Hansen and Lange argue it 'better capture[s] the market rhythms of pit trading prior to its demise' and 'offers a means by which to understand how pit traders' bodies are calibrated as metronomes of market rhythms' (2015: 1087). The reader encounters the central character of Cutis Jadwin (based on well-known trader, Joseph Leiter), Page Dearborn (the sister of the protagonist's wife-to-be), and Landry Court (a broker's clerk) and their different positions in relation to the market are used to explore the grip of its rhythms. Page remains too distanced from the workings of the market to properly assume its rhythm. Despite being 'in a position similar to Lefebvre's idealized balcony' since she has not previously been grasped by the rhythms of market life, she can experience it only as 'noise and chaos' (Borch, Bondo Hansen and Lange 2015: 1087-8). In contrast, Landry can '"feel" the market ... almost at his very finger tips' (Norris 1994[1903] in ibid.: 1088). This alignment of mind and body is triggered when trade commences, and he instantly experiences a heightened attentiveness. It gives him an edge but also puts him at risk as the rhythms of the market threaten to overtake such a zealous trader. We see this most clearly in Cutis' obsession with wheat which is the source of his rise and later his downfall. In this instance, capital is destructive. It penetrates everyday life and finally destroys it, just as Lefebvre tells us it will.

A different stance towards the allure of market rhythms discussed by Borch, Bondo Hansen and Lange is the tradition of 'contrarian speculation' developed in prescriptive American trade literature in the 1920s and 1930s. The contagious affective charge of the crowd meant markets were perceived as potentially 'deceptive' and contrarian traders would not therefore take them at face value. Instead, they sought to achieve balance between participation and observation, trusting neither their own bodies nor those of other traders. The techniques they developed to 'remain unaffected' and to avoid impulse buying included to 'fixate one's attention' for instance by writing down their observations of the market during trade.[5] The aim was 'to calibrate, in a literary sense, the body as a metronome of the market, in a manner that focussed attention on the market rhythms without the individual becoming *mentally* subsumed by the rhythms' contagiousness' (2015: 1089, emphasis in original). Borch, Bondo Hansen and Lange discuss contrarian speculation in terms of the separation of distinct 'bodily' and 'mental' rhythms which they say is not systematically tackled by Lefebvre. I read this differently. Lefebvre calls on rhythmanalysts to think with the body (2004: 21): the body itself and mental processes are not detached from one another. Indeed, Lefebvre's rhythmanalysis is, following Chen (2017), a phenomenological approach in which there is no separation between mental, physical and social aspects of being (Merleau-Ponty 2012[1945]). While there are varying cognitive frameworks through which practical understanding may be rendered – and different reflexive techniques such as fixating one's attention may help here – mental processes themselves cannot occur separately from the body situated in place and time.

High-frequency trade

The world of HFT is quite different from life in the pit and requires some contextualization. The closure of trading floors in stock markets across the world was set in motion by legal changes and technological developments in the latter part of the twentieth century.[6] The first shift was to 'screen' trading where traders work in designated trading rooms engaging with the market via screens and the click of a mouse. However, there has been a second and fast-growing shift in the past decade or so 'characterised by an intensified computerization of markets' where trade takes place in a 'fully digital space' (Borch and Lange 2017: 284). HFT is a subset of this shift to algorithmic trading and now accounts for more than half of all financial trades. This has implications for financial stability, social crisis and insecurity and there have already been a number of flash or sudden crashes (Thompson 2016: 2). HFT also sheds light on the '*algorithmization of society*' more generally which is happening across a range of sites from social media to dating (Borch and Lange 2017: 303, emphasis in original). Little is known about how finance firms and markets operate and secrecy within these

---

[5] They have much in common with ethnographers here.
[6] For instance, what came to be known as the 'Big Bang' in the London Stock Exchange on 27 October 1986.

firms may actually be part of a protectionist strategy to prevent imitation and shield capital (Lange 2016). However, such technologies may 'prompt new ways of acting and thinking in markets' (Borch and Lange 2017: 284) and new ways of apprehending rhythm.

In HFT, algorithms – that is 'the practice of organizing a set of instructions to execute a decision that can be rendered into an electronic computable form' – are central. Trade takes place through the interaction of algorithms with one another as they seek to anticipate 'proper' prices and transact accordingly (Thompson 2016: 2). This happens at speeds beyond human capacity – in tenths of a second up to microseconds – and firms pay significant sums to locate physical infrastructure (servers, cables, etc.) so as to minimize execution times and thereby get an edge on their competitors.

Traders are spatially isolated from one another in HFT trading rooms that usually accommodate seven to ten desks. Each trader is literally surrounded by screens running the codes of their different algorithms. Traders' bodily proximity to one another in the pit is replaced by proximity to their screens. Visibility is no longer key. On the contrary, some have partition walls and privacy filters to conceal codes. Traders have two sets of screens. One set depicts market rhythms through the 'electronic limit order book, showing the bid and ask prices' but the trader is generally not concerned with these. The other set, comprising as many as six screens, shows the trader's algorithms, codes and graphs of performance and these are the focus of their attention (Borch, Bondo Hansen and Lange 2015: 1090–1). Borch and colleagues learnt about these machinic relations through the direct observation of the traders' working spaces. They asked questions about what was going on in 'real time' but noted that responses were often partial, either because discussions were interrupted by the demands of the algorithms or because traders were reticent to speak in front of one another. What talk there is in the trading room generally concerns code, software and algorithms rather than markets. Indeed, value is attached to the efficiency of code rather than understanding of market developments and company performance in real terms – although some traders do take part in informal exchanges in chat rooms trying to discern who is trading what, where and when (Thompson 2016: 3). It is significant that the majority of the predominantly male traders are highly educated mathematicians, computer scientists, physicists and engineers rather than economists or finance specialists (Borch and Lange 2017: 292, 294).

While traders might be understood as watching the market and its effects rather than acting within it (Zaloom 2006: 6 in Borch and Lange 2017: 287), HFT is not without human intervention. Direct bodily immersion in the market to gain access to its rhythms is not possible since the rhythm of the market is not 'compatible with a human timescale'. So, instead, traders '*calibrate their bodily rhythms to their algorithms* (and thereby *indirectly* to markets)'. They monitor and amend their algorithms intensively, switching them on or off or substituting one for another as market conditions change. This requires 'close physical-bodily proximity to the algorithms' as well as phone applications which alert them to trouble when the human needs for rest and breaks impose themselves and take them away from their desks (Borch, Bondo Hansen and Lange 2015: 1091–2, emphasis in original).

It is clear that the rhythm of the market has increasingly become out of synch with cyclical body rhythms. Borch, Bondo Hansen and Lange argue that this happens in two ways: through *extension* and *intension*. Extension refers to the market's temporal reach, and intension to the speed of HFT. Futures markets for instance are open twenty-three hours a day. Traders work long hours and in shifts to successfully oversee the operation of the algorithms. They must trust one another, a particular burden for the algorithm's writer-creator who may feel considerable emotional attachment to it (Lange 2016). Night traders frequently fall asleep at their desks or use 'optimising' substances to better calibrate and indeed modify their bodies and sleep patterns to the algorithm's own rhythms and its unrelenting enforcement of linear time (Borch, Bondo Hansen and Lange 2015: 1091–2). The hour that the market is shut is no time for rest either. It takes discipline not to intervene to adjust algorithms based on short-term emotive impulses and this gives rise to considerable psychological complexity. Market absorption is clearly not the goal in HFT (Borch and Lange 2017: 296, 301).

The rhythms and temporal reach of the working day of the HFT trader are strongly driven by the operation and needs of the algorithms themselves. While there is a cyclical rhythm to their maintenance (from constant to every couple of weeks) and replacement (every three to six months), this takes extended and linear working schedules to be accomplished. However, there are many instances when this linearization is suspended. When economic announcements are made for instance, traders consider it too risky to gain from the unpredictability that follows and wait for it to pass instead. Trade is also interrupted by the cyclical rhythms of the weather as the microwaves that permit high-speed transmissions are susceptible to rain and other atmospheric interferences which limit their performance in linear time. This suggests that even in the case of such a technology in the forefront of capitalist processes, Lefebvre's emphasis on the colonization of the cyclical by the linear needs to be nuanced (Borch, Bondo Hansen and Lange 2015: 1092, 1094).

Finally, it is interesting to consider what the rhythms of high-frequency trade might mean for the production of gendered differences and identities in these settings.[7] As in pit and screen trading, HFT is very male-dominated. However, the temporalities and social relations of these working practices are significantly different. While pit and screen traders are known to work, play and socialize intensively in highly sexualized and gendered ways which Linda McDowell has documented so well in *Capital Culture* (1997) – and a spate of legal cases attest to[8] – high-frequency traders must work intensively *and* extensively. This calls for and produces different types of subjectivities and capacities. Gendering rhythmanalysis might offer new insights into the gendered relations of rhythm in the forms of trade discussed here, and the relevance of rhythm in the production of sexual difference more generally.

Reflections

Borch, Bondo Hansen and Lange have demonstrated the usefulness and limitations of rhythmanalysis for studying the everyday operation of capitalism in financial markets. In HFT, the speed of trade is beyond human perception. However, instead of giving up on rhythmanalysis because the body is no longer central, they show that rhythmanalysis can be done differently attending to constellations of bodies, material (screens) and immaterial (algorithms) elements that mediate the trader's relationship to the market. Being in the zone is no longer about bodily presence but about being 'algorithmically present in markets in order to be able to sense their rhythms and proactively adjust the strategies on this basis' (2015: 1093). Yet, the efficacy and success – or indeed failure – of the algorithms operating at extreme speed in HFT are accumulated over weeks or months rather than in days or minutes. There is a certain slowness then to the HFT trader's

---

[7] Borch and colleagues make reference to gender in their published work but state that it is not the focus of their attention.
[8] See Ellen Poe's *Reset: My Fight for Inclusion and Lasting Change* (2017).

work compared with the pit or screen trader in a 'paradoxical inversion of time horizons' (Borch and Lange 2017: 293–4, 302).

In the discussion of pit trade above, we heard how contrarian speculators considered that the body could not be trusted. In HFT, we learnt how the body is not central to market processes; so rhythmanalysis needs to take place through other tools. In the following example, we continue thinking about the means by which we might access and examine rhythm if the senses cannot always directly read the moves and rhythms of the market or interpret them clearly. The next section considers, contra Lefebvre, the value of the audiovisual for doing rhythmanalysis.

Example three: The insufficient body: Using audiovisual methods to capture rhythm

The third set of examples showcases the development of rhythmanalysis through audiovisual methods. In his Foreword to the second edition of *Critique of Everyday Life*, Lefebvre is explicit in his recognition that some forms of film and cinema 'reveal a truth about everyday life'. He discusses Charlie Chaplin and the 'secret of his comic powers' which do not reside in the body itself but 'in the relation of this body to something else: a social relation of the material world and the social world'. Chaplin's *Modern Times* is widely recognized as showing the rhythms of bodies at work under capitalism, the pace set by the machines at odds with the rhythms of Chaplin's body and tempo which he dramatizes with great hilarity, tragedy and insight. In relation to his early films, Lefebvre commends Chaplin for constructing 'a fiction truer than reality as it is immediately given' (2014a: 32, 35).

In *Rhythmanalysis* itself, Lefebvre seems to have mixed feelings about the use of the audiovisual. He is open to recording sounds when he writes:

> The theory of rhythms as such has received solid support from the possibilities of reproducing rhythms, studying rhythms by recording them, therefore of grasping them in their diversity: slow or fast, syncopated or continuous, interfering or distinct. Putting an interview or background noises on disc or cassette enables us to reflect on rhythms, which no longer vanish whenever they appear. (2004: 69)

However, he is less convinced of the power of the visual to apprehend rhythm: 'no camera, no image or series of images can show these rhythms', he states (2004: 36), despite being able to view them with the naked eye from his balcony. To a twenty-first-century reader, however, with the 'unprecedented opportunity' (Back 2012: 18) of a vast range of everyday devices quite literally to hand, this position is too constraining. Indeed, Lefebvre's insistence that 'the rhythmanalyst calls on all his senses' (2004: 21) actually chimes with stances adopted by researchers who seek to tune into the environment using visual and sensory techniques and technologies as supplement to or an extension of embodiment in immersive and non-representational ethnographies today (see Pink 2015).

Several scholars have employed audio/visual methods to undertake rhythmanalysis, often in an experimental way.[9] While taking inspiration from Lefebvre, Alan Latham and Derek McCormack nevertheless take issue with his insistence on the 'body as a metronomic sensory apparatus' and the only way to access rhythm. On a field trip to Berlin with cultural geography students, they found that far from being a 'technique of distancing or detachment', visually documenting interaction with a camera in urban space made apparent the rhythms of everyday sociality on public transport for instance. Working with images may therefore be a method for 'thinking through the rhythms of urban environments' (2009: 252, 256–7). Also based on recordings in Berlin, Michael Pryke (2000, 2002) constructed audio and photomontages to document 'the white noise of capitalism' in the rhythms of the global economy as they can be seen and heard in the newly created Potsdamer Platz and to evoke place-making through time. Tom Hall, Brett Lashua and Amanda Coffey worked primarily with sound by making recordings as they shadowed night workers in the city of Cardiff arguing that sound provides 'clues to the rhythms of an urban everyday' and a means 'to open up ... polyrhythmic complexity' (2008: 1028). James Evans and Phil Jones take this a step further, listening rather than solely looking at scientific data in their creation of a short film to 'make non-human rhythms palpable' in their work on the socio-natural rhythms of the city. They use rhythmanalysis to 'reveal, capture and resensitise' the set of rhythms that characterizes urban socio-nature (2008: 663–4).

---

[9] Including Whyte (1980) to document small urban spaces, if not with a particular focus on rhythm.

In the discussion of Tim Edensor's work earlier in this chapter, video and photography were elements of ethnographic-rhythmanalytic observation and documentation. Paul Simpson (2012) makes use of time-lapse photography to capture movement, interaction and rhythm in the public performance of a street magician.[10] Time-lapse is an interesting technique as rhythm is inherent in the pulse of the sequence of images produced between what is seen and not seen (Jungnickel 2015). The shift from one image to the next is visible to the human eye unlike in the flow of images in film and video.[11] For Simpson, time-lapse provides an opportunity to record 'the *qualitative* unfolding of events as they happen' (2012: 31, emphasis in original) and is a means to perceive the variety of rhythms that permeate them as the researcher can subsequently play with time by accelerating or slowing the sequence of images in the process of analysis.

Documenting the rhythm of a fish market

In what follows I present my own study of London's Billingsgate fish market (Lyon 2016[12]) in which I created a montage of time-lapse photography and sound in order to explore the ways that rhythms intersect, coexist and clash. In autumn 2012, inspired by Henri Lefebvre's call to attend to rhythm and as part of a broader project on the fish industry, I embarked on a visual ethnography of the market. Trade at Billingsgate officially starts at four o'clock in the morning, but fish merchants and salespeople can be seen setting up from around one o'clock. Although fish cannot legally leave the market before 4.00 am, serious buyers, mostly for the hotel and catering industry, would have often browsed the samples on display and already made their decisions by then.

Arriving in the early hours, I deliberately wandered around the market hall letting myself get caught up in or 'grasped by' the rhythms, noises, tensions, buzz, chill and thrill of the place, hanging out with fish merchants, inspectors, porters and traders. I shadowed different workers and took numerous tea breaks in one of the cafes or, when I got the chance, with the fish inspectors. Good relations in the market were essential for obtaining

---

[10] His videos can be viewed here: https://www.youtube.com/watch?v=GjiwHwsX9L8 and https://www.youtube.com/watch?v=fGjDn-IQRL0

[11] There are twenty-five frames per second in film.

[12] Material from this section is taken from a longer discussion in Lyon (2016). The final, definitive version of this paper has been published in Sociological Research Online, 21/3, August 2016, All rights reserved. © SOCIOLOGICAL RESEARCH ONLINE.

formal and informal acceptance for the project and for the film – and for the ethical conduct of this research. The cultural tone of the market, characterized by banter and playfulness, structured many of my own interactions and added to the pleasures of being there. I was welcomed as a guest (Gherardi 1996), conspicuous as a relatively young woman in socially homogeneous space dominated numerically and culturally by older, white, working-class men. If I was treated with paternalism, there was no shortage of displays of 'competitive' masculinity too (Kerfoot and Knights 1993), performances mostly for and between men.

Whenever I arrived at Billingsgate, I felt myself absorb the atmosphere as 'spatial bearers of moods' (Böhme 1993: 119), transforming the experience of temporality – was I really this lively at four o'clock in the morning? And by the time I left the market, I had a sense of having been there *accumulated* through time. But in the hours that I spent there, I noticed that I kept looking over my shoulder. I came to think of this as a bodily expression of the uncertain sense of where exactly the market was happening, of its 'perpetually forming and deforming atmosphere' (Anderson 2009: 79). It's as if the market comes to life behind your back then slips away before you had the chance to take it in, I often thought. Immersion in the market was it turns out an obstacle to perception of its rhythms (Lefebvre 2004: 28, Borch, Bondo Hansen and Lange 2015: 1085).

The idea of making a film based on time-lapse photography came out of this sense of the intangibility and sensory excess of the market space and offered a mode of documenting and rendering the temporal structure of the market. The architecture of Billingsgate provides a particular opportunity for seeing its 'temporal unfolding' (Simpson 2012: 431) from the vantage point of a gallery at either end of the first floor overlooking the market hall, akin to Lefebvre's balcony. The market hall is central to the everyday life of Billingsgate as a space of display, interaction, movement, negotiation and exchange, and it is where trade can be observed. I repeatedly found myself climbing the stairs and looking down on it from the first-floor gallery, taking stock of the mood and patterning of the day's activities. It was here that the concrete possibility of making a film based on time-lapse photography began to take shape. My body and senses were clearly instruments of this research (Turner and Norwood 2013), especially in alerting me to the dispersed feel of the market and sparking this way of apprehending market space, but they were insufficient to capture the polyrhythmic complexity of the place.

With a film-maker/collaborator, Kevin Reynolds,[13] I chose one night in December 2012 to record the scene.[14] Just after midnight, we set up two digital cameras (one as a backup) in the first-floor gallery location looking down the length of the market hall above one end of the central aisle. This position allowed us to look along as well as down on the market floor, the perspective emphasizing a viewpoint into the distance and proximity in the foreground, conveying a sense of immersion. The composition suggests the continuity of the space beyond what can be seen in the foreground and so keeps the viewer located within and not wholly above it. Most of the frame is taken up with the market floor, reaching up to the level of the clock suspended from the ceiling in the centre of the market hall, which also offered us the opportunity to explicitly mark clock-time for the viewer. This framing is a deliberate choice which heightens the unitary sense of place and the intensity of what goes on there. But it is a particular view. Another location, up high within the market space looking down on it from a bird's eye view or at floor level would certainly have conveyed a different sense of space (Simpson 2012: 430).

We took photographs from just before one o'clock in the morning until midday, from market setup until the market hall was (almost) still. The interval between photographs was ten seconds, based on Kevin's technical judgement and my preferred aesthetic that this would not mask and excessively 'smooth' the conditions of making the film. The depth of field allowed everything in the frame to be kept in focus. The fire glass against which the lens was pressed (and held in place with tape) is visible, also evidencing the making of the film, and situating the camera and the viewer in place. The sound of the market hall is muted in this gallery location but every hour (at varying times within that hour) I went down to the market floor to do some 'soundwalking' (Hall, Lashua and Coffey 2008). Slipping into the flow of the crowd I made brief recordings on a handheld digital recorder of whatever sounds were in my path.

The resultant film – or audiovisual montage, stills from which are shown in Image 3.3 – is a combination of a selection of the sounds I recorded

---

[13] Kevin Reynolds runs veryMovingPictures: http://verymovingpictures.co.uk/ [accessed 17 March 2018].

[14] I obtained formal consent from the City of London Corporation and informal verbal consent from the tradespeople in the foreground of the frame to make the film and gave them an opportunity to comment on a preview before making it public.

Image 3.3 Stills from Billingsgate Fish Market, Dawn Lyon and Kevin Reynolds, 11 December 2012: https://www.youtube.com/watch?v=nw_kf32GfHY (Author's own images).

with the sequence of images speeded up so one hour is presented in thirty seconds. This is a deliberate calibration based on judgement and experimentation that this speed would both distil patterns and flows and immerse the viewer in the experience of the space. The rhythms of the space that I could sense were present were made visible by increasing the speed of the images. Once the speed and thereby duration of the film were settled, we edited the sound bites. We started at four o'clock in the morning, synchronizing the sound of the bell that signals the beginning of trade with the visual that shows the clock striking four, and worked backwards and forwards from there. This was a 'creative-analytic process' in which we sought to evoke Billingsgate with an 'affective force' that goes beyond representation (Garrett and Hawkins 2015: 145–6).[15]

The construction of the montage is explicitly artificial. If we accept that all methods help to produce the reality they study (Law and Urry 2004), this deliberate undertaking to render rhythm does not diminish the significance of the presence of rhythms in the real-time flow of the everyday. Since such rhythms are hard to grasp in their immediacy, montage offers an effective 'medium of anthropological [or ethnographic] inquiry' (Grimshaw 2011: 248) and 'a tool of multi-sensory and affective discovery' (Garrett and Hawkins 2015: 147) or a means of *doing* rhythmanalysis. It creates 'mentally prolonged spaces' in which attention is repeatedly renewed, 'a sort of meditation on time' (Lefebvre 2004: 33, 30). By losing the richness of the detail, we sidestep the sensory overload that live presence and video entail, and begin to distinguish some threads among this 'temporal, material, technological and cultural tangle' (Sharma 2014: 4). As from Lefebvre's window, 'the flows separate out, rhythms respond to one another' (Lefebvre 2004: 28).

The film both describes rhythm and does 'a distinctive form of analytical work' (Grimshaw 2011: 257). It exposes the polyrhythmic complexity of the market and evokes a 'sense of time as motion and transformation' (Crang 2001: 201). In particular, time-lapse delivers the 'spatio-temporal unfolding of everyday events' over a duration (in linear clock-time) and reveals 'how various rhythms and routines interrelate and interfere' (Simpson 2012:

---

[15] Since making the film available on YouTube: https://www.youtube.com/watch?v=nw_kf32GfHY, it has (at the time of writing in July 2018) been viewed over twenty-two thousand times. At the market, reaction to the film was marked by pride in what workers saw as a positive representation of their working lives and community.

440), for instance as different workers occupy the space, from sellers and buyers to cleaners. Indeed, through the film, I was better able to explore the relationships between rhythm, atmosphere and mobility, and interconnections and interactions in market space which I discuss below.

Perceiving rhythm through the audiovisual

On the night we photographed the market, we tried to get to Billingsgate ahead of anyone starting work on the market floor. Despite arriving at midnight, we were not the first there. But we did get a feel of the place when it was still and quiet which the film conveys, especially in contrast to what follows. It was chilly – minus three degrees centigrade outside, and at least as cold inside – and the first sounds of preparation for the day can be heard clearly, echoing in and marking out the space around.

Day breaks inside the market hall from the left of the screen as the bright lights get switched on for traders to set up ahead of daylight seeping in from the outside when the sun comes up. The colours become more vivid, first dominated by the yellow of the overhead structure, the green of the floor, then the white of the trader's clean coats. By three o'clock in the morning, the lids are lifted on sample boxes of fish which are carefully placed on display. The glistening combination of skin, scales and ice adds to the intensity of the morning brightness and spectrum of colour. It's a new beginning and there's a sense of anticipation in the air.

Telephones start to ring, and the sound of the market hall imposes itself. Once it is set up for trade, the soundscape is intense, sometimes jarring or confusing as multiple rhythms compete for attention. It's possible to discern 'layers' (Makagon and Neumann 2008) as we hear the close ring of a telephone, someone shouting nearby, or the pervasive squeak of the polystyrene boxes being moved around. Walking around the market – the way we made the sound recordings for the film – accentuates this.

The mood quietens by around eight o'clock in the morning as the market is 'undone' and its charge dissipates. The navy, black and red of the buyers' clothes are replaced by rubbish bins and containers in bright blue, grey and orange. The main lights are switched off at around ten o'clock and we see daylight from the roof windows reflected in the floor, wet from the washing down of the stands. It's quiet again, with just the final cleaning to finish off. Those ringing in from the outside don't seem to be aware of these rhythms.

While I asked questions of merchants and tradespeople about the length and organization of the working day, I would argue that the film is a more powerful statement of the 'rhythmic production of space' (Pryke 2000), and the pace and excitement of market life (Dixon and Straughan 2010: 455) than quotations from interviews. In it we see 'different temporal itineraries that constitute social space'. The presence of the clock at the top of the images emphasizes variation in the intensity of work, the duration of different tasks and activities, and the tiring repetition across whole stretches of time, enhanced by the mesmeric quality of time-lapse. It also hints at 'the complexity of lived time' and the 'micropolitics of temporal coordination' with the world outside Billingsgate such as two-shift sleeping, calculated convergence with others' lives, patterns in which some bodies recalibrate to the time of others (Sharma 2014: 5–7, 20).

The 'sense of time' (Vannini 2012a: 243) of Billingsgate in a broader set of urban and natural rhythms is also evident once the market is still for the day. It's a contained world when trade is at its peak, but once the inside lights are switched off and daylight is seen reflected in the wet floor, the viewer recognizes the rhythms of the market as being at odds with the city space around it – an instance of arrhythmia. What we cannot observe however is the anticipation of rhythms that are beyond the present that make the market happen the next day, and the one after – orders placed and deals done in processes that extend well beyond the temporal frame of the film. A different kind of design attentive to the temporalities of these rhythms would be needed in order to grasp them.

The architecture of the market hall is very clear from the vantage point of the film, especially the central aisle which produces the encounters within it as customers 'walk' the paths made for them (Harvey, Quilley and Benyon 2002: 206 on Covent Garden), the 'verges' lined with fish. There are around fifty traders at shops or stands – some beyond the frame – back to back in four 'corridors' lengthways with several cross-cutting paths at intervals along them. The green of the floor indicates public space, the space belonging to the stands demarcated in dark red. These boundaries are fluid however, as buyers step behind the displays to make a more private deal, and boxes and trolleys encumber the main paths.

The relative immobility of the sales staff and merchants contrasts with buyers on the move. Groups form and scatter, like an uneven pulse, stimulated by sounds or gestures or the lure of the fish in ways that the film does not allow us to appreciate at a micro level. Indeed, there are multiple coexisting rhythms when trade is in full swing. While there is some jostling at the stands, what is striking is that this destabilizing of the boundaries between self and other leads to an *accommodation* of bodies in space and a *fluidity* of the movement of the crowd (Dixon and Straughan 2010: 454–5) – a synchronization enhanced by the speed of the film. This includes the movement of porters in the market hall facilitated by cries of 'mind your legs', '... your legs!' and the rumble of trolleys. The porters manoeuvre their loads skilfully, or cope with how their loads gain momentum – the trolleys have no brakes and cannot easily be stopped – acting as 'pacemakers' (Parkes and Thrift 1979: 360) in the market space. Customers and other workers familiar with the market are tuned in to 'sensory information about the physical and social environment' (Dixon and Straughan 2010: 449) and smoothly and spontaneously move out of the way. The visitors on tours of the market with Billingsgate Seafood Training School stand out for their lack of bodily comprehension of the space – as did I at first. But I soon absorbed the rhythms of market life, an instance of Lefebvre's dressage, to 'bend oneself (to be bent) to its ways' (2004: 39).

Lefebvre argues that space is produced and enacted through physical gestures and movements (Merrifield 2000: 177), and that rhythms inhabit the body can be seen very clearly at Billingsgate. Workers are tuned into the environment around them through their bodies and their senses, to one another, and to their working tools and materials (Hockey and Allen-Collinson 2009). There is a 'transpersonal dimension' (Anderson 2009) to how they work together, coordinating tasks and movements (Lyon and Back 2012: 5.12) through a non-reflective practical knowledge. The sound track of the film also alerts the viewer to the materiality of the market. The squeak of the polystyrene boxes is omnipresent. The boxes resist being lined up closely together, protesting loudly at times, and neither are they quietly acquiescent when picked up by porters wearing gloves or with wet hands. While each noise is not necessarily rhythmic, their overall clamour makes us pay attention to the materiality of work, to the nature of the objects that occupy the working space alongside people and fish.

The rhythms, movement and intensity of the market change through the night. The fish merchants and salespeople move around fast but steadily when the space is clear, until they are slowed by the presence of the fish which leads to more uneven rhythms – darting here and there, squeezing past obstacles, negotiating with things on the move. At the ring of the bell at four o'clock in the morning, which signals the legal start of trade, there is a subtle shift in speed and activity on the part of traders and buyers familiar with this repeated daily marker of official time. Movements gather pace and the pace gathers. We feel the polyrhythmic character of the market, including those stretches marked by a repetitive monotony. There is a linear character to the market, from preparation through to the sale and closing and cleaning up when the market is over, portrayed in the film by the steady and swift movement of the hands of the clock at the top of the frame. But there is more. The institutional rhythms of clock-time may structure the working night and day but the market is not characterized by this linearity alone. Alongside these lines through time, recursive loops, 'repetition, rupture and resumption' (Lefebvre 2004: 78) in an 'always emergent interaction' of linear and cyclical (Simpson 2008: 823) interfere with one another. We see and hear the cyclical repetitions of the sale and the movement of fish. We notice the differentiated rhythms of buyers and sellers and the temporalities of different types of work activity in harmony or at odds with one another.

Reflections

We can see through this example how rhythmanalysis 'provides a practical vocabulary' (Simpson 2008: 823) for research on the rhythms of market life – both in the traditional setup of Billingsgate and in the case of HFT presented in the previous section. It helps to generate new understandings of the 'rhythmic ordering' (Simpson 2012: 424) of work, and the specific way in which 'time makes space into place' (Parkes and Thrift 1979: 353) in the market. And it offers a research strategy for doing rhythmanalysis which has the potential to be applied in other fields. However, this particular mode of doing rhythmanalysis also obscures some of the temporalities of market life. Most obviously, the image of the market hall framed by the film is limited and does not inform viewers of the other processes and multiple temporalities that underpin the movement of fish through Billingsgate. We cannot see anticipation for instance, except for how it is inferred from the accommodation of moving bodies in space from one moment to the next. Yet my narrative interviews with fish merchants and salespeople reveal how multiple forms of anticipation and future-thinking are part of the everyday experience of work. Traders actively think about matching buyers and sellers when they make decisions about what products to offer, they plan in terms of seasons and holidays, and manage the vagaries of the weather and regulation and their implications for supply. It is therefore important to recognize that any one rhythmanalytical research strategy may be insufficient to grasp the full workings of rhythm or that rhythmanalysis may be one strand of a research design that uses different tools to address different aspects of a study.

Conclusions

The aim of this chapter was to deepen the discussion of the practice of rhythmanalysis through projects which have developed Lefebvre's approach in different directions. In the first section based on the work of Tim Edensor and colleagues, the body is a privileged tool to directly observe, feel and register rhythm as a means to analyse mobility and place-making. However, the body is also deployed in conjunction with other instruments of data collection including narrative interviews, diary-writing, film and photography. These studies present rhythmanalysis as a flexible approach which blends embodied and sensory research with talk, text, sound and image. Questions remain about whose body registers which rhythms and what this means for the production of knowledge – and these are further addressed in Chapter 4.

In the second and third examples, the body is not centre stage. In their work on the rhythmanalytical practices of high-frequency traders, Christian Borch, Kristian Bondo Hansen and Ann-Christina Lange reveal the workings of capital *in* the everyday so disassembling Lefebvre's strong opposition between capitalism and everyday life. Within this, traders' bodies are found to be calibrated to their algorithms in contrast to earlier, corporeal and place-based forms of trade (see also Snyder 2016). However, such forms of trade persist, as in the case of my own study of Billingsgate fish market. Here the body was important to feel the presence of multiple coexisting rhythms, but alone it was an insufficient instrument to detect and disentangle them. Instead, audiovisual methods – time-lapse photography and sound recordings – provided a means of perceiving and presenting rhythm.

The working patterns of high-frequency traders, and buyers and sellers of fish as well as the night cyclist in Cook and Edensor (2017) all draw attention to working – and leisure practices – at night. There is a well-established literature that documents the social significance of the broken and disrupted sleep of shift-workers and the consequences for bodily and mental health (e.g. Snyder 2016, Wolkowitz 2006). More recently attention has been focused on the 'ruinous consequences' of 24/7 capitalism (Crary 2013) and its demands for temporal coordination (e.g. Sharma 2014, Wajcman 2015) as its reach extends. These arguments certainly chime with Lefebvre's concerns and fears for the colonization of the everyday by linear over cyclical rhythms. However, in the examples discussed in this chapter, colonization is neither total nor always unidirectional. Rhythmanalysis offers a means to articulate and refine the relations between the cyclical and the linear and gain new insights into the ways we live.

4 What is rhythmanalysis good for? Some gains, limitations and future directions of the rhythmanalytical project

Introduction

In Chapters 2 and 3 I considered Lefebvre's conception of rhythmanalysis, the range of fields in which it has been applied empirically and the diverse ways it has been developed methodologically. In particular, the discussion critically explored doing rhythmanalysis where the body is a central tool of research as exemplified in the work of Tim Edensor; where the body is present but displaced as effective rhythmanalysis requires attention to bodies *in conjunction with* material and immaterial elements of work, as in the analysis of high-frequency trade conducted by Borch, Bondo Hansen and Lange; and where the body is necessary but insufficient and audiovisual methods are employed to do what the body alone cannot to register and perceive rhythm, as in the case of my own work on Billingsgate fish market.

This chapter brings the critiques of the earlier discussions together, extends and deepens them, and considers future directions for rhythmanalysis. It is organized around four main areas. First, I discuss different practices of embodied and sensory research bringing Lefebvre's recommendations into dialogue with current ideas. The second topic is time. Here the discussion is on rhythm as a neglected form of temporality in relation to other temporal concepts. It further explores how rhythmanalysis might inform a better grasp of temporality and spatiality in research design and methods including the potential of 'synchronization' and 'disruption' as research tools. The third area concerns the scale and scope of rhythmanalytical research. A strength of rhythmanalysis is its applicability to a wide range of settings and questions. Here the reflection concerns its scope more explicitly and what it offers as a mode of inquiry at and across different scales. The final section is on communicating rhythm. The discussion draws on examples which showcase different modes of representation – and modes beyond representation – through which research on rhythm can be conveyed, including in visual, audiovisual, sonic and written forms.

Rhythmanalysis as embodied and sensory research

There is a sense in which the rhythmanalyst *becomes* rhythm as the body's own rhythms combine with the ebbs and flows of other people's actions and interactions and the liveliness of the material world in which they are immersed. When I think now of walking across the market hall at Billingsgate shadowing a porter on the way to collect orders from one of the adjoining chill stores, what I recall is the reach of my stride mirroring his. I absorbed his rhythm. It was a stretch for my (shorter and smaller) body but meant I registered this walk at a kinaesthetic level in relation to my usual pattern and pace. This happened in a similar way in relation to different senses as I followed the gaze of the fish inspector with my own eyes, simultaneously asking him to describe what he was seeing and how he was looking, or when listening closely to the interactions of sellers and buyers on the market.

The rhythmanalyst seeks to inhabit the rhythms of others with his or her own body, tuning in to others' movements and gestures, attentions and anticipations, letting different rhythms make themselves felt. Beyond the moment or situation rhythm is noticed through the difference its absence makes. In this process, the rhythmanalyst's body is mobilized 'as a set of rhythmic relations through which the spatio-temporal turbulence of everyday life registers as so many intensities of feeling' (McCormack 2013: 42).

The body is clearly a tool of rhythmanalytical research as we saw earlier in the discussion of Lefebvre's and others' practices (Chapters 2 and 3). It is also an object of research in rhythmanalysis as attention to the relations between bodies and environments reveal the body's capacities to act (Kullman and Palludan 2011: 350). Such corporeal relations in the research process are well recognized by embodied ethnographic researchers (Perry and Medina 2015, Turner and Norwood 2013). Feminist scholars in particular have called for an appreciation of knowledge as 'situated' (Haraway 1988) in time, space and known through the body, notwithstanding the complexities of acknowledging difference while resisting essentialist categories of biology and identity. However, despite the centrality of the body as a tool and object of rhythmanalytical research and the theoretical sophistication of embodiment in the current literature, the linkages between the actual flesh and blood, breathing and feeling body of the researcher and the experience of being in the field are often only faintly drawn. I noted this earlier (in Chapter 3) in relation to some of the work of Tim Edensor and colleagues but want to make a stronger point about it here.

There have been some important developments for empirical enquiry in the social sciences in recent years which are relevant here. Non-representational or more-than-representational theory or theories as it is variously called emerged in geography as a way of thinking which foregrounds practice, especially embodied practices, process and materiality (Thrift 2007). It recognizes the 'excess' of social life beyond our capacities for perception, conscious awareness and representation; it emphasizes so-called pre-cognitive aspects of life in everyday practices; and it promotes an open-endedness in accounts of the world. However, this focus on embodied practices does not always extend to a reflexive consideration of the researcher's body doing research; instead it continues to privilege the cerebral despite its acknowledgement of the corporeal. Mike Crang refers to this as a 'ghostly absence' in geography (2003: 499), a point previously made by others, notably Judith Okely (1992, 2007) with respect to anthropology.

Some of the literature on rhythmanalysis and time space more generally which puts the body centre stage also disregards important feminist scholarship since the 1980s. Discussions of affect for instance do not always give due regard to the contribution of work on emotion, embodiment and place, much of which was undertaken by women at a time when such concerns were marginalized (Pedwell and Whitehead 2012). I would argue that rhythmanalysis can do this differently. And since it relies on accessing intimate details of embodied experience to be done well, it needs to aim high in terms of the standards of its practice. If we use our bodies to perceive the world as a research strategy, the simple recognition that different bodies perceive differently implies taking account of who is doing what, to what end and with what effects. Embodiment can be mobilized as part of a reflexive process to unpack the relationship between researchers' own histories and capacities and the ways these inflect the production of knowledge from design to interpretation, however complicated and varied this might be (Nencel 2014,[1] Parker 2016, Peake 2016, Rose 1997, Wright 2010).

The body is not a singular entity and the operation and deployment of the senses is important in any embodied research practice (Hockey and Allen-Collinson 2009). But standard sociological tools – the survey and the interview for instance – deal poorly with the fleeting, the distributed, the multiple, and especially the sensory, the emotional, and the kinaesthetic, as Law and Urry argue (2004: 403–4). In recent years, visual and sensory methods have emerged as part of broader move across the social sciences to 'engage the senses' (Pink 2005), offering a way of retaining the vitality and dynamism of the social world in our accounts of it (Back 2007, Back 2012, Back and Puwar 2012). The aim here is not to reproduce the social world as we encounter it but not to deaden it with the concepts, methods and style of the social sciences. Visual methods – still and moving images – have perhaps been at the forefront of the rise in sensory research and despite the dangers of overstating the significance of vision in everyday urban life in particular and in the construction of objects and sites of research, used imaginatively they remain valuable as in some of the examples already discussed (for reference see also Back 2007; Bates 2015; Harper 2012; Mitchell 2011; Pink 2005, 2007; Rose 2016; Spencer 2011; Wills et al. 2016). While the content of images may assist rhythmanalysis, the practice of doing research with the camera can also sensitize researchers to the embodied and material (Hunt 2014).

Lefebvre advocated cultivating the 'attentive ear' (2004: 27) in particular and for rhythmanalysts to learn 'to listen to a house, a street, a city, as one listens to a symphony or an opera'. Moods, he says, are more important than specific images, atmospheres more relevant than spectacles. We have encountered examples already that explicitly explore music in urban space and rhythm as something which is embodied and experienced in sound (Bull 2000, Moore 2013, Labelle 2010). Sonic methods more generally seem to be gaining ground as a sensory approach in part as an important counter to the dominance of the visual in accounts of urban experience (Biddle and

---

[1] 'How to be reflexive will depend on the objectives of the research, the type of knowledge produced, the position of the research subject in the broader society and the particularities of the research context' (Nencel 2014: 75).

Thompson 2013). Below I briefly discuss two examples of the use of sound in rhythmanalysis.

George Revill (2013) argues for a more reflexive and active sense of listening than Lefebvre envisaged. Using psychoanalysis and the work of philosopher Jean-Luc Nancy, Revill focuses on listening rather than hearing. Although he does not explain exactly how he goes about this, in his account of listening to rhythm in a railway station he argues that this enables him to appreciate the station as a space of creative and imaginative possibility rather than simply one of linear regulation which a strict reading of Lefebvre might suggest. A second example is the study of bodily rhythms in festival spaces where Michelle Duffy and colleagues (2011) extend Lefebvre's thinking to highlight how the body senses rhythm and thereby inhabits it in space as well as rhythms inhabiting the body. This is made clear in the comparison of two festivals in Australia. In each, the researchers deployed their own bodies as research instruments, they kept research diaries to bring the operation of rhythm into conscious awareness, and they conducted swift on-the-spot interviews with parade participants. Whereas in the Swiss-Italian festa, participants were 'infected' with rhythm, in the ChillOut parade rhythm was 'diffused or lost' as 'its rhythmic flow was less than predictable' (18–22). Other senses – of smell, taste and touch, or the haptic (e.g. Paterson 2009) – are also important for rhythmanalysis if trickier to work with directly. Tim Schwanen and colleagues' (2012) 'smellscapes' for instance suggest routes through urban space, and reinforce the character and feel of a place (Degen 2008: 45). Lefebvre is contradictory on the olfactory. On the one hand, smells and scents act 'as traces that mark out rhythms', he says; on the other, 'odours seem not to obey rhythms' (2004: 21, 41) but there is clearly potential for creative research practices here.

What then does working with the sensory in the practice of rhythmanalysis add up to? Chen conceives of rhythmanalysis as a 'meta-sense'. Since rhythm is grasped at the level of the sensory she argues, 'rhythm is a *meta-sense* which synthesises bodily and extra-bodily impressions' (2017: 2). It is a *dispersed* kind of sensing. It is experienced at the level of bodily consciousness, recognizes how a sense of rhythm is shaped by the intangible and appreciates that rhythm is not bounded by the body. Chen argues we need to further develop a vocabulary for 'practising rhythmanalysis' which can speak to this 'temporal-spatial consciousness' and sensitivity to rhythm, and help cultivate critical, imaginative and creative possibilities in research.

Indeed, rhythmanalysis works well with the non- or more-than-representational, tuning into mood and atmosphere as Lefebvre recommends and sensing the pre-cognitive in everyday experience as bodies affect and are affected in their encounters (Kullman and Palludan 2011: 350). That said, the talking and reflecting body is still of interest to rhythmanalysts and many of the examples discussed in this book include combinations of collecting talk and text alongside the sensory. As mentioned earlier in the discussion of Tim Edensor's work, perhaps talking about rhythm can produce rhythmic talk revealing the operation of rhythm in the ebb and flow of an account. Rather than Lefebvre's suggestion that rhythmanalysis might replace psychoanalysis, rhythmanalysts might instead learn from psychotherapeutic practices (as narrative analysis and psycho-social approaches have done, for example Hollway and Jefferson 2013) to recognize rhythm in talk.[2] Here too it is important to be reflexive and transparent about the process by which one set of voices gets translated into another in the authorship of rhythmanalytical research. This chimes with James Ash and Lesley Gallacher's (2015) calls for a 'vocabulary of embodied methodology' that captures sensory experience beyond the boundaries of the body. They advocate 'becoming attuned' in order 'to increase our capacity, as researchers, to sense difference'.

Rhythm for thinking and researching time and space

Throughout this book, I have sought to demonstrate how working with rhythm and practising rhythmanalysis can generate insight into spatial and temporal relations within and beyond the everyday. Lefebvre's rhythmanalysis is not of course the only way to pursue this aim. In Chapter 1, I briefly discussed the time space geography developed in Sweden in the 1970s. In the last decades of the twentieth century and into the twenty-first, geographers, philosophers, sociologists, anthropologists and legal scholars have conceptualized time and space in various novel ways. Rhythm is a component of the philosophers, Gilles Deleuze and Félix Guattari's (1987) 'refrain' (*ritournelle*) as a passage, communication or coordination between spacetimes which produces familiarity (Crespi 2014;

---

[2] Susie Orbach discusses just this in *In Therapy* (2016) and 'The Poetry of Therapy': https://www.theguardian.com/books/2016/oct/29/susie-orbach-poetry-of-therapy

McCormack 2013: 80) – and this has been taken up widely by geographers. Rhythm features in Barbara Adam's 'timescapes' (1998) and Edward Soja's (2010) discussions of spatial justice and notably in contributions by Nigel Thrift (and colleagues) to thinking time space (Amin and Thrift 2002; May and Thrift 2001; Parkes and Thrift 1979; Thrift 2007).

Rhythm is considered to be a useful basis for a conceptual methodology for cultural theory and Henriques, Tianen and Väliaho (2014) argue for a new conceptualization of rhythm as vibration, a force of the virtual and intensive excess outside of consciousness. Several scholars have made use of rhythmanalysis in conjunction with other conceptual resources. For instance, Stanley Blue (2017: 3) proposes a combination of rhythmanalysis and practice theory to shed light on 'processes of institutionalisation' and 'to capture the interconnectivity, multiplicity and complexity of social phenomena'. In particular, Mike Crang (2001, 2005) makes use of Mikhail Bakhtin's concept of 'chronotypes' originally devised for the analysis of fiction to consider space, time and the relationship between them, together with Lefebvre's rhythmanalysis (Mulíček, Osman and Seidenglanz 2014: 310).

Whatever the conceptualization of time and space in a project, it has implications for research design. For working with rhythm, Lefebvre advises: 'In each case the analysis should ride with the movements in whichever work or whichever sequence of actions until their end' (2004: 15–16). I read this guidance as twofold. First, it is important to undertake a preliminary rhythmanalysis of a site, an activity or the unfolding of an event to identify the rhythms that are present. Second, it is these rhythms which then inform the research design. In Rob Smith and Tom Hall's (Hall 2010; Smith and Hall 2013; Hall and Smith 2014) study of urban outreach workers, their recognition of the cyclical character of rhythm and its duration in the city informs their 'twenty-four-hour design'. In a similar way, my own work on Billingsgate fish market through the night (Lyon 2016) registers rhythm through a complete cycle – albeit one embedded in broader cycles – of the life of the market from midnight to midday. Where and when we target our attention is a central consideration of rhythmanalysis – and of ethnography more generally, as Paul Atkinson points out (2015).

Time-use studies[3] have long provided fascinating data about the 'quantities' of time people devote to different tasks and lead to important

---

[3] See Centre for Time Use Research, University of Oxford: https://www.timeuse.org/

insights, for instance about cross-national variation in the gendered division of domestic labour. However, the conceptualization of time that underpins this research programme is linear, expressed in terms of the clock. Temporality is not chronology, Ingold reminds us (2000: 194). Chronometric time both misses the lived experience or 'texture' of time (Flaherty 2011) and what Mark Harvey (1999) calls 'economies of time'. Economies of time suggest that the coordination, sequencing and articulation of work/ other activities produce particular temporalities – and rhythms. This can be seen at a macro level in his analysis of the economies of time in France and the UK. Similar ideas can also be explored at a micro level. Ben Snyder (2016, discussed in Chapter 2) develops a rhythmanalytical research strategy which allows him to gain a deep understanding of the rhythmic relations of everyday working lives. He explores *synchronization* in time and *sychorization* (coordination in space) among three groups of workers subject to the disruptions of flexible capitalism: financial professionals, truck drivers and unemployed job seekers. Snyder uses his own 'embodied thick description' of the intertwining of time and space to grasp rhythm. He is 'able to ride with drivers for multiple consecutive days and mirror their sleep/wake rhythms so that I could better understand the physical demands of delivering freight', he writes (21). He experiences directly how the delivery 'involves the transmutation of one set of rhythmic patterns into another set of rhythmic patterns using the vigilant body as a medium' (107). And he observes how the driver 'experiences economic exchange in his body' (123).

Lefebvre and Régulier point out how we largely become aware of our rhythms 'when we suffer from some irregularity' or disorderliness (2004a: 77). Indeed, disruptions and crises have 'origins in and effects on rhythms', Lefebvre notes. They produce a kind of 'hole in time' which can be filled by a creation or an invention (Lefebvre 2004: 44).[4] While Lefebvre was keen to see the transformatory potential of these 'cracks' and openings in the flow of spacetime (his 'moments' discussed in Chapter 2), he argues that *disruption* reveals rhythm, rendering visible what was previously unnoticed and under the surface. 'The value of disruption' is as a site of politics and a space of possibility for newness, different actions and interventions;

---

[4] There's some similarity with the Situationist idea of *détournement* here as a 'reversal or hijacking' of accepted norms (Merrifield 2006: 34).

and it is also a 'heuristic device' for doing research into rhythm (Edensor 2000: 135-7).

The ethnomethodology of Harold Garfinkel (1917-2011) already offers a long-standing sociological tradition of suspending the taken-for-granted to expose the workings of social life and power, often through 'breaching experiments', concrete interventions in social situations. Rhythmanalysts might be attentive to disruption as it arises or, as in ethnomethodology, provoke it as a research tactic.[5] Breakdowns and shortages are part of everyday life. They reveal its spatio-temporal fragility and 'offer a snapshot of rhythms as they unravel' (Trentmann 2009: 69). For instance, Stephen Graham discusses how the vast urban 'infrastructural circuits' of the west come into view when volcanic ash or power cuts make the uninterrogated background of everyday life 'startlingly visible'. He concludes: 'Infrastructure disruptions also present a major opportunity to understand cities better' (2014: 469-71).[6]

Others have explicitly sought to go against dominant rhythms in order to detect them as in some of the examples previously considered. For instance, Bowdler dances on a footbridge as people awkwardly attempt to pass her (Edensor and Bowdler 2015). Students stand still in a crowded stairwell in the *U-bahn* so as to sense (and film) the flow of the crowd (Latham and McCormack 2009: 5-7). And Degen, DeSilvey and Rose (2008) intervened in the space of a shopping mall to stimulate the reactions of passers-by. *By The Way* (1999), a journey undertaken by the artists, Tea, offers some novel ways of documenting and displaying disruption. The journey from Liverpool to Hull was made by car moving between four hotels and recorded in real time with a video camera pointing out of the passenger window. Each time the car came to a stop as a result of the rhythms and regulation of the traffic, a member of Tea took a photograph of that location. Once this initial journey was complete, Tea returned to those locations and asked people to comment on the places in the images. These commentaries (seventy-six of them) became the sound track to the video and excerpts are transcribed on the reserve

---

[5] Ethical considerations are especially important here. Indeed, it is worth remembering that disruption is central to flexible capitalism with its emphasis on 'improvisation over planning' (Snyder 2016: 5) and is commonly used by IT companies ostensibly to stimulate creativity and innovation.

[6] See: http://www.teaweb.org/by-the-way.html

Image 4.1 Concertina journey by Tea, *By The Way*, 1999 (with kind permission of Peter Hatton).

of the relevant photograph. The still images were published in concertina format, a section of which is shown in Image 4.1. If disruption reveals, it also creatively transforms (Revill 2013: 62) and the experience of the repeated journeys of *By The Way* were themselves shaped by the process of documentation and research. Such forms of exploring the rhythms of time and place also highlight their uneven production (Hubbard and Lilley 2004), in turn making researchers more attentive to apparent 'interruptions' both in the production and the viewing of images such as these.

The scale and scope of rhythmanalysis

Lefebvre was hugely ambitious for the significance of rhythmanalysis – nothing short of a new science, he asserted (2004: 3) – as well as for its empirical reach. It certainly lends itself to historical analysis and perhaps most readily to the detailed examination of the social at the scale of the everyday. Indeed, the previous chapters have discussed numerous examples of research which traces rhythm in the home, on the street, across the city and at work. These studies mostly use methods which are more commonly associated with ethnography, and rely on the body of the researcher as direct observer or supplemented by recording devices which mediate, extend or enhance its sensory apprehension. However, while rhythmanalysis can be said to have alliances with ethnography, it is not wedded to a singular method or restricted to qualitative approaches more generally. DeLyser and Sui (2012) argue that it cannot be captured within a qualitative– quantitative divide, and this chimes with broad understandings of time and space as both measurable and comprehensible through subjective experience. Indeed, rhythm 'reunites **quantitative** aspects and elements, which mark time and distinguish moments in it – and **qualitative** aspects and elements, which link them together' (Lefebvre 2004: 8–9, emphases in original).

Rhythmanalysis as conceived by Lefebvre was intended to cut across multiple scales, from the bodily to the cosmic (Simonsen 2004). In Chapter 3, we saw the rhythmanalyst as observer of the body-screen-algorithm amalgam through which rhythm operated. While the body remains relevant in this instance, are there other examples where methodologically it is further displaced? For instance, what methods can we use for grasping the global rhythms of travel, information technologies or flows of online communication (see Clough et al. 2015; Tinati et al. 2014)? What happens when the rhythms that are of interest for research exceed the body's capacity for enquiry? What kinds of research questions can and cannot be addressed? Chen (2017) argues that at the level of research design, instead of looking for classic agents that produce specific rhythms, we must instead identify and explore 'sites of rhythmic production', rhythmic 'assemblages', 'bundles' or entanglements. Studying rhythm therefore means studying social processes such as multiple interconnected interactions which themselves give rise to rhythms.

GPS technologies offer one set of possibilities for exploring rhythm. They have been used to amalgamate multiple individual datasets and expose routes in urban spaces for instance but face a challenge in not reproducing the kinds of rigid descriptive representations of the early days of time-geography (Hägerstrand 1970). One interesting example that sidesteps this danger is from the UrbanDiary project which includes a comparison of personal mental maps with GPS records. Such a methodology may not be feasible with large samples (Neuhaus 2010: 325) (although novel uses of big data are on the rise (Birkin 2018)). In an innovative development, Beverley Skeggs and Simon Yuill (2016) make use of rhythmanalysis with 'big data' to question how Facebook structures social relations and monetizes energies. As in the case of Borch, Bondo Hansen and Lange (2015) investigating capital's everyday from the position of high-frequency trade, Skeggs and Yuill 'get inside' one of 'capital's new lines of flight' (2016: 1356). Using bespoke software to study software as well as more conventional survey and interview tools, they produce data visualizations which expose patterns of interactions in time if not in space, notably in relation to Facebook's sponsored stories, advertising and newsfeeds. Their research process was 'not entirely straightforward' (ibid.) but opens promising new directions to explore rhythm at a bigger scale.

Conveying rhythm

Doing research through embodied, sensory, performative, visual or haptic means has been marked by innovation and creativity in all sorts of ways in recent years as discussed at the beginning of this chapter. Researchers have vastly expanded the range and character of the tools of their trade, making a real difference to the ways in which qualitative research in particular can 'get' how other people's lives take shape. However, the ground gained in what are effectively modes of data collection has not seen parallels in the forms through which research can be communicated and these remain limited. In this final section, I discuss what conveying rhythm might demand of researchers – and publishers – and explore the potential of some imaginative and experimental developments across different fields.

First, let's not give up on writing. While the written word is often criticized for deadening the liveliness of the social world, it doesn't have to be this way. Les Back calls for sociology to be a more literary craft 'informed by a commitment to patience, accuracy and critical judgement'. There is no letting up on the robustness of the research process here, only a hope that the result might lead to more 'artful description' and analysis (2007: 21). Ben Snyder's work does this well. In a passage entitled 'A Long Night' (2016: 103–8), Snyder waits with Alvaro, an owner-operator of the truck he drives to collect a load of frozen chicken. Snyder's writing conveys frustration, patience, mounting tension, stillness, resignation, uncertainty and the multiple recalibrations of the body necessary in relation to the unknown end point of the wait. In the meantime, the clock ticks: 7.00 pm, 8.33 pm, 3.32 am, 5.08 am …. It weighs heavily. I don't realize until they pull away from the poultry plant that as a reader I too have felt the strains and rhythms of the night.

Kathleen Stewart gained the attention of readers across the social sciences and humanities with the publication of *Ordinary Affects* in 2007. The book is entirely composed of vignettes of ordinary life in the form of stories, detailed observation and critique without offering an overarching analysis. In an entry entitled 'Odd Moments', she starts: 'At odd moments in the course of the day, you might raise your head in surprise or alarm at the uncanny sensation of a half-known influence' (2007: 60). Here she catches something that can't easily be put into words but is expressed between these lines and the reader's familiarity with such moments. Anna Gibbs (2015) – who also discusses *Ordinary Affects* – argues for a form of critical writing that refuses to be contained by the injunctions of the academy. For instance, poetry might work for rhythmanalysts to make use of form as well as meaning to convey rhythm as, following Henri Meschonnic (1982), it is 'the mode of discourse closest to the body' (Gibbs 2015: 233).

While writing remains important, researchers also have other means at their disposal in today's mediated world – as we saw in the discussion of Billingsgate fish market in Chapter 3 and in some of the examples above. Philip Vannini (2012b) considers the non-linear, multi-modal (for instance, text, image and sound) web-based possibilities for sharing research that evoke and move readers and viewers beyond a cognitive register of informing them. In addition to creating bespoke websites, spaces for web-based publication are growing (e.g. *Journal of Video Ethnography* and *Sensate*[7]). Anthropologists have been at the forefront of advancing alternatives to text or new ways of working with text (Cox, Irving and Wright 2016; Elliott and Culhane 2017; Pink 2005; 2007). Lucien Castaing-Taylor stands out for forging novel modes of evoking everyday life through the audiovisual. I am thinking in particular of his film *Leviathan* (2012) with Véréna Paravel which through cameras situated on different parts of a fishing boat immerses and disorientates the viewer (almost to the point of sea-sickness!) and brilliantly renders the fierce and expressive rhythms of life at sea for the fishermen bound up with the water, the boat, the fish and other sea life, as well as being subject to the movements of the sea itself. While the form relies on sound and image, Pink (2007) argues that video in particular appeals to multiple senses, not least since the senses themselves are connected so that we might '"read" touch, smell and taste' from audiovisual images (Merchant 2011: 66).

Criminologist and film-maker David Redmon also undertakes experimental audiovisual ethnography 'that crafts sensory knowledge from aesthetic experience'. In *Mardi Gras: Made in China*, for instance, he shows 'temporal, topographical, and corporeal connections' as the viewer sees 'the repetitive movements of a teenage worker with red scars on her fingers from sewing beads' which he contrasts with 'the repetitive exchanges of beads transacted through revellers' hands' (2015: 433–4). No one does it better than David Hockney though. His *The four seasons, Woldgate Woods (Spring 2011, Summer 2010, Autumn 2010, Winter 2010)* multi-screen video work shown simultaneously on four walls of a square room immerses

---

[7] *Sensate*: http://sensatejournal.com/

the viewer in an environment that reconfigures time as the video shows the camera moving along the same stretch of road across the seasons of the year.[8]

Other visual forms developed explicitly to show rhythm include Filipa Wunderlich's juxtapositions, layered photographs and 'spectral diagrams' (2008, 2010, 2013). Wunderlich's work is visually rich and evocative and the photographs she positions alongside one another are effective for identifying and showing different 'place-rhythms'. Images from her 'Freeze-time photography project' use different moments in time superimposed on one another so the viewer sees the same figure more than once in a single frame, for instance a few paces apart, and thereby gathers a sense of their movement through time and space (as in the work of photographer, Pelle Cass). Her spectral diagrams are an interesting attempt to combine different data (sound, image and movement). However, while formally rich, they risk losing their capacity for communicating the sensory when put together in a two-dimensional form in print. In addition, Joe Graham (2015) has developed an arts practice drawing technique to record the *moving present* as a means to reveal rhythm.

If sound is especially appealing to rhythmanalysts for registering rhythm, it is also a form in which rhythm can be conveyed, either from recorded sonic data or through the transformation of other data into an audible form, and there are some exciting developments in this field (see Gallagher and Prior (2014) for a review and future directions). In particular, Michelle Duffy, Gordon Waitt and Theresa Harada (2016) have devised what they call 'visceral sonic mapping as a research tool'. They repeatedly listen to their recorded sounds and annotate them in the form of a 'sound map', gradually adding the distinctions and interconnections between different layers of sound.[9] In an ethnography of driving, they also shared these maps with research participants to trigger the emotional and affective resonances of the sounds for them. For instance, in 'Trevor's drive', the specific ways in which he drives *with* and not just *in* the car surface through this process (55).

Michaela Palmer and Owain Jones (2014) face a different challenge as the rhythms they are interested in, such as tidal patterns of the Severn Estuary in the west of England/south of Wales, are not directly accessible

---

[8] For a glimpse of the work, see: https://www.ngv.vic.gov.au/multimedia/the-four-seasons/
[9] Examples can be accessed here: https://soundcloud.com/search?q=sonic%20geographies

in audible or other sensory forms. Taking inspiration from Evans and Jones' (2008) aural representations of environmental data in a transdisciplinary application of rhythmanalysis across the human and non-human,[10] they undertake a procedure of 'sonification', converting data from environmental processes into sound.[11] Sonifications identify and apply sounds to processes and rhythms and produce 'maps' which can be 'redrawn' in flexible ways. They make non-human rhythms that are usually beyond the reach of human apprehension available to the human senses and 'retain the liveliness of an event' (Palmer and Jones 2014: 225). This is a particularly fascinating application that has potential for diffusion across other fields. Finally, Eleni Ikoniadou (2014) also considers the 'rhythmicity' of the event at the margins of perception in an analysis of digital media art practices and experiments.

At this point, I hope the reader will appreciate what rhythmanalysis might be good for as an open-ended approach which operates in time and space at different scales attempting to grasp, analyse and render the rhythms of the social world in meaningful ways. In the concluding chapter, a worked example exposes in some detail the thinking behind a new rhythmanalytical project.

---

[10] The published article is a transcript of the film which can be viewed here: http://www.blackwell-compass.com/home_video#gecofilm
[11] Their website, Sonic Severn, and examples of their own and students' work are available here: http://www.sonicsevern.co.uk/about.htm

5 What is rhythmanalysis? Conclusions

> **Notes towards a 'how to' guide: Doing rhythmanalysis over dinner**

Writing a book has its own rhythms. It involves intense work and pauses. For me, the breaks include regular Friday night dinners at my local Italian restaurant – and discussions of where I am at in the writing. It's January 2018 and the readers' reports have come in. They are mostly positive and offer constructive suggestions for improvements. Their strongest criticisms are levelled at the conclusion. I sit and consider them with my partner. 'How would you do a rhythmanalysis of this place?', he asks. I can always be drawn on this question. As we talk, it strikes me that *La Cucina*[1] could be just the setting to finish this book.

In what follows, I talk through a possible dinner at *La Cucina* (composed of real elements but from different occasions) and use it to formulate questions for a flexible *working guide* to doing rhythmanalysis intended as 'enabling' or 'sensitizing' (following Willis and Trondman 2002: 394). I draw out how rhythmanalysis as a research strategy prompts the researcher to take particular directions. The account shows how it shares ground with what an ethnography of the life of this restaurant might attend to as well as how rhythm inflects such a study differently. In this worked example I outline the multiple ways researchers can orient themselves to be attuned to rhythm.

I'm excited now as the restaurant emerges in a new light. I've thought about this casually before but stopped short of appreciating the polyrhythmic complexity and interconnections of eating and cooking, socializing and serving made possible through repeated preparations and performances across the years. Restaurants 'provide a valuable experimental site to study space and time' not least given their 'rigid temporal and spatial pressures'

---

[1] A pseudonym.

(Demetry 2013: 577) and offer an opportunity for doing rhythmanalysis in an 'ordinary' space. Established twenty years ago, *La Cucina* is locally owned and popular. It presents itself as offering simple, tasty, traditional and authentic Italian cooking in a welcoming atmosphere at a reasonable (mid-range) price. Opening hours are fixed, with lunch from 12.00 pm to 3.00 pm and dinner from 6.00 pm to 10.00 pm with some variation at the weekend. As I sit there, I try to hold in mind the different temporal and spatial scales implied in the production of the sequence of food I will eat tonight. First questions might be: What is the reach of this subject in time and space (cf. Knowles 2014)? Where and when might a study of it take place?

We are always greeted warmly.[2] Then the question: 'Have you booked?' is both an injunction (you should have done) and an offer of latitude (we understand, we will try to make room for you anyway). The last time I made a reservation, I was told we had to choose between a 6.00 pm or 8.00 pm sitting. This is new; perhaps an effort to corral unruly consumers into slots that suit the rhythms of the kitchen and the management of the restaurant floor. And it inspires new questions: What different rhythms can be identified in the restaurant space? How do these rhythms relate to one another? Which positions (in time and space) and roles does the researcher need to adopt to grasp them?

I'm looking at the menu now and trying to settle on what to eat. The pizza here is good. The oven is close to the entrance so it's brought to mind as soon as we walk in, a sensory intervention in the rhythms of appetite. But it's Friday and my years in Italy have left their mark which means that the timing doesn't feel right as I learnt to think of Sunday night as pizza night. Not that anyone cares about this in Kent. In any case, I know I will struggle to digest it. My own bodily rhythms are not made for the heady combination of fat (cheese), gluten (dough) and acid (tomatoes). These thoughts make me aware of how different cultural practices and bodily rhythms underpin the dinner I will end up consuming. Put more generally: How is a meal shaped by cultural practices associated with time and place, custom and

---

[2] I started going to *La Cucina* as a lone diner several years ago when my house was being refurbished and the kitchen was out of use. The rhythms of Italian-style eating enabled me to 'territorialise time' over dinner and the impression of welcome from the staff gave me a 'feeling of belonging' which assured my repeat business (Lahad and May 2017: 1.3, 8.3).

biography? How do social and cultural rhythms make themselves felt? – or how are they resisted – at a bodily level?

Tonight we want to linger. Italian-style eating is generally a structured affair. We start with antipasti – one to share as we're hoping to make it through all four courses. *Calamari fritti*? Better in summer perhaps. Or we could go straight to a *primi* (first course)? I make a case for sharing *melanzane alla parmigiana*: the layers of aubergine, cheese and tomato are just the thing on a wet winter night. We might ask: What is the relevance of broader temporal patterns for action in the present? How in particular do seasonal rhythms shape decisions and actions?

Next up are mushroom ravioli. There's a backstory to this dish that takes my mind in another direction. True or not, the tale is told that the ravioli are handmade by somebody's grandmother, evoking a world of slow food and traditional (if stereotyped) practices. Still, this raises another question and one which has a different reach: What are the rhythms, practices and norms that underpin the production of the food emerging from the kitchen? I'm hungry tonight (all the more so in the interests of this imagined research) so opt for a *secondo* (main course). There's recognition that diners might not make it this far so we haven't ordered this course in advance. We pause to consider the menu once again and the earlier interaction is repeated. At this point I wonder: What are the possible (multiple but limited) rhythms of consumption in the restaurant? What do these imply for the management of the restaurant space in and through time, and the organization of work more generally? How do they shape different patterns of interaction between customers, staff and kitchen workers?

Perhaps it's time to look at the situation from a different point of view. In his collection of essays on *The Mind at Work*, Mike Rose interviews his mother about her experience of waitressing. She gives an extraordinarily rich account of the polyrhythmic complexity of waiting on tables – if not formally expressed in those terms. Rose is curious about how as a waitress, his mother (confusingly, also called Rose!) displays her ability to 'think on her feet' (2004: 2). It suggests a grasp of the mood, pace and rhythm of each table and the restaurant space as a whole as something that is felt or sensed and quickly understood. Looking around me at *La Cucina*, it is clear that the job requires attention and agility in decision-making and action. Thinking on one's feet implies no opportunity for reflection. Rhythm informs and inhabits the invisible and tacit skill of this work. We might ask: What are the competing rhythms that underpin the work of 'waiting'? How are they absorbed into the body? And in what ways can these be accessed directly or indirectly by the rhythmanalyst?

'Thinking on her feet' is no metaphor for the work of the waitress. Her 'bodily skill' (Rose 2004: 8) is apparent in her reactions because she has grasped the rhythm of her work through practice. Learning arises initially through watching others. That's evident in *La Cucina*. A group of staff – men and women, mainly Sicilian – can be seen to watch and wait. They are agitated with the bodily tension of anticipation and then they are off, darting to this table or that, swivelling back as another customer calls, moving quickly to the kitchen for a late request. They are mostly on the move and never doing just a single task. *Coordination* is central to their work which is closely connected to rhythm (King and de Rond 2011). The demands of restaurant service are not only for *synchronization* at a single moment in time (e.g. meals served to the same together together) but for *succession* through time. The sequence, pace and timing of tasks as a set of coordinated activities produce the rhythm of what is a collective social performance. Waiting staff use their bodies to tune into the multitude of competing rhythms that permeate restaurant spaces. The rhythmanalyst might do the same, literally undertaking waiting work to grasp its demands and tensions across the mind and body.

Anticipation, concentration and memory remain essential to keeping things ticking over smoothly in a restaurant but there are tensions. Waiting staff work to the linear time of the clock while diners consume according to the cyclical rhythms of their meals, the nature of the occasion and their own propensities for eating quickly or at a leisurely pace. The time pressure of the worker must be experienced as the relaxation of the customer. Or perhaps the diner is in a rush and anxious to get through a meal and this is counter to the rhythmic norms of the kitchen and the service. What instances of arrhythmia can be found in restaurant settings? How can different configurations of rhythms be characterized, especially between the front and back stage of the restaurant?[3]

There's an explicit division of labour at *La Cucina*. Waiting staff bring menus and take drinks orders but food is the domain of the managers (one per shift on a weekday, two at the weekend). They set the pace and direct

---

[3] The study of waiting work has a long history. Erving Goffman developed his ideas of front and back stage in part through his observations of waiting staff in the Shetland Hotel (1959: 120, 169).

staff to tables they sense need attention, choreographing this collective performance in time and space. It's possible to observe them using their 'skilled vision' (Grasseni 2004) and other senses to tune into and manage the atmosphere and conduct the work. This offers the rhythmanalyst an opportunity for observation and a basis for asking questions of them. This setup also conveys that the managers are responsible for ensuring customers are kept happy and unusually perhaps they appear to perform a large share of the emotional labour of the dining experience, at least that perceived by the customer. How then do the managers act to ward off the arrhythmic threat of complaint for the affective atmosphere of the restaurant? How does this impact on their own working rhythms and those of the other restaurant workers from floor to kitchen?

There is usually a 'peak period' in the course of the evening when there's a heightened atmosphere of conviviality, fluid interactions and tempting food emerging at just the right moment (or not). Our food arrives as we are ready for it – the rhythm is smooth and steady tonight. There is enormous judgement and skill that underlie this pacing. What is going on behind the closed doors of the kitchen to make this happen? Gary Fine's *Kitchens* based on ethnographies of the social and institutional worlds of restaurant kitchens can shed some light on this (and I am indebted to him here). He asks: 'How is synchronization achieved? What organizational procedures promote this competence?' (1996: 61).

Each order starts a new rhythm for the chef and staff need to be in synch within and beyond the confines of the kitchen itself. Although digital ordering is now commonplace with menu choices sent directly from the table, at *La Cucina* waiting staff write down orders and take these to the threshold of the kitchen, if not any further. Chefs then assess the timing of the multiple tasks facing them.[4] Since they are usually catering for groups, specific combinations of dishes must converge from different trajectories of preparation to be ready to serve together. If inexperienced chefs rely on clock-time, their seasoned counterparts have incorporated a more embodied sense of 'timing' which shapes the rhythm of their work.

[4] The temporal reach of the preparation of meals started much earlier when orders for ingredients were placed, and on the day itself in the partial preparation of dishes on the menu. Chef biographies (a genre in itself) and reality TV programmes give a sense of what this is like. It's first thing in the morning and Anthony Bourdain, still in bed, recounts: 'I'm thinking triage – sorting in my head what gets done first, and by whom, and what gets left until later' (2000: 183).

In addition the food itself has temporal properties (as well as spatial requirements) which means there is a shorter or longer 'temporal window' in which to make different dishes. Duration can be 'squeezed' or 'stretched' through adjusting the tempo or speed at which food is prepared. Still, as one of Fine's interviewee's comments, a piece of fresh fish is no longer that if it's 'wrecked' through overcooking (Fine 1996: 73–4, 78–9). Since the kitchen is noisy from the combination of voices and the material clatter of pans and plates, it's hard to directly perceive rhythm with the senses (ibid.: 65). The rhythmanalyst must find other means: analysing a single dish perhaps, retracing how it was made after the event through narrative accounts as well as in situ observation.

There are several dimensions of temporal and spatial adjustment or 'recalibration' (Sharma 2014) necessary in restaurant work. Kitchen staff must calibrate their actions in relation to the temporal bodily demands of customers who must in turn accept the norms of and pacing of food preparation as a social practice and the spatio-temporal properties of their menu choices (the prevalent 'please allow an extra 15 minutes for chocolate fondant pudding' for instance). Waiting staff must tune into the rhythms of the kitchen to do their own work; and they may simultaneously pressure chefs and cooks to sustain the rhythms of the tables they are serving. What then are the 'micro-politics of temporal coordination' (Sharma 2014: 7) and the power relations at play in getting a plate to the table? How do different regimes of power shape the experience of time and space for restaurant workers and customers? The rhythms or discordances of talk between different restaurant workers might also be illuminating here – notably as kitchens are famed for strong language and emotional intensity (Demetry 2013; Fine 1996) – and offer rich data for rhythmanalysts.

In her observation of a restaurant kitchen, at first Daphne Demetry 'was perplexed where to stand' and this alerted her to the challenges and practices of bodily accommodation and coordination in such a space. Eventually she found that being on the move and working informally allowed her to be caught up in the flow of movement and feel the rhythms of kitchen work with her own body (2013: 584). She also noticed the contrasting ways in which different chefs positioned themselves to orchestrate the flow and rhythm of work. Similarly, Fine explored how the physical environment of the kitchen affects what cooks do. Despite discipline in the organization of work, there was corporeal 'friction' among

Conclusions   101

kitchen workers who 'frequently bumped into each other' (1996: 80–7). Further, the frustrations of having to work with poor quality equipment were widely discussed as chefs experience everyday accidents such as cuts and burns that result from the spatio-temporal pressures of the job. What, we might ask, does the restaurant environment do to workers' bodies? How do they experience the demands of being on their feet in relation to the body's rhythms of activity and rest? How does kitchen work as a collective activity engender its own rhythms (cf. the boat race discussed by King and de Rond 2011)?

We're onto dessert now which is simpler than the previous courses as most of the traditional options – *tiramisu, panna cotta, gelato* – have been prepared ahead of time. It's getting late. There's always a moment when we realize the restaurant has been winding down and we have only just noticed (cf. Billingsgate fish market discussed in Chapter 3). The heat of the pizza oven that steamed up the windows earlier has left trickles of cold condensation in its wake. I also start to see that the restaurant decor has faded in places, hinting at other rhythms of maintenance and repair.

The rituals of settling the bill and saying goodnight are the final moments in the rhythm of the dinner and we step outside. As we walk along the street, I am struck by all this brief discussion has not considered. Who were the people eating in the restaurant and how did they come to be there? What are the macro connections in space and time – both proximate and distant – that make possible having dinner here tonight? I am now wondering about ordering and the scale of anticipation required for different kinds of food stuffs and menu changes over time. And more broadly still, about the cultural and sensory appeal of Italian cuisine in the UK and the circulation of people, products and practices that sustain it. When I walk past the restaurant in the afternoon on other days, I notice the preparation that is being done when the 'closed' sign is up. I think about the intersection of the different rhythms of chefs and cooks, kitchen and waiting staff, delivery people, cleaners and customers. And so on.

Albeit incomplete, this worked example shows how rhythmanalysis is powerful for tracing connections between the micro-rhythms of one meal and the spatial and temporal patterning of restaurant work and the industry more generally. It enables us to explore rhythms within rhythms and identify different interlocking configurations of rhythm. By bringing the often taken-for-granted spatial and temporal dimensions of the social world to the fore in an interconnected way, rhythmanalysis makes possible different forms of analysis and critique of everyday life as the examples in this book have revealed. The centrality of time and place in this approach generates new understandings of social life as it unfolds, cutting across different scales.

Final remarks

This book has explored some possibilities of working with rhythm and I hope that readers can now more readily imagine what rhythmanalysis offers them in understanding their own everyday lives and the worlds they research. While rhythm remains 'both evasive and porous' (Morris 2017: 7), the book has sought to counter the sense that however present, it is difficult to discern and isolate. It has set out some means by which we may grasp the simultaneous entanglement of various rhythms (Lefebvre and Régulier 2004a: 77) which threaten to disappear when considered too closely. It has shown how and when rhythmanalysis can be used as an approach to document, analyse and understand the complexity of time and space and everyday life in capitalist society. 'Sooner or later', Lefebvre states, 'the analytic operation simultaneously discovers the multiplicity of rhythms and the uniqueness of particular rhythms' (2004: 16). And it has demonstrated the practice of rhythmanalysis as both 'practico-sensory and intellectual', conceptual and corporeal (McCormack 2013: 42).

For Lefebvre, rhythm is not a place or a thing but an interaction; it is energies in flux arising from a relationship between space and time. The social world and social practices are composed of rhythms which combine different forms of linear or cyclical patterns and repetitions with novelty and difference (1991: 206). Lefebvre's body of work was a critique of capitalism and any application to other social, economic and political systems needs to be carefully considered. That said, rhythmanalysis can be used to heighten awareness of the radically uneven power relations of globalization (Alvarez 2007: 70). Furthermore, if rhythm is a 'process through which subjectivities are managed' (Henriques, Tianen and Väliaho 2014: 15), might thinking with rhythm open the way to new temporal practices, to conceiving of new ways of living, working and being in the world? Elaine Stratford's *Geographies, Mobilities, and Rhythms over the Life-Course* explores 'how life's potential and our capacity to flourish are wrapped up in varied rhythms, mobilities and geographies' (2015: 11). And

James Evans (2010) spells out the urgent need to develop new rhythms to live by in relation to the changing ecological context of the twenty-first century and the dominant linear conceptions of time which inhibit our capacity for anticipation.

At the same time, we need to guard against the ominous potential of rhythmanalysis and the captivating appeal of rhythm itself. If in traditional soldiering practices, the drill leads to the 'euphoric fellow feeling' of 'muscular bonding'[5] (McNeill 1997: 2) it also contributes to the creation of strong armies and the exercise of violence and destruction, while the deployment of military drones in the twenty-first century using rhythmanalysis is more sinister still (Henriques, Tianen and Väliaho 2014: 16). In everyday life, 24/7 surveillance and discipline on the street, online and on the body (through wearable technologies) augment the reach of governing through rhythm (Davies 2018). However, the solidarity and community that emerge through the rhythms of cooperation (King and de Rond 2011) have progressive potential, and arrhythmia – literally being 'out of step' with the dominant regime – may offer a spacetime of resistance (Davies 2018).

Finally, notwithstanding the challenges of accessing research funding and the politics of knowledge production, the present day is an exciting time to be developing methods which help researchers arrive at nuanced understandings of social, political and cultural life (Back 2012). The title of Shaw, DeLyser and Crang's (2015) article, 'Limited by Imagination Alone', suggests and promotes space for researchers to explore and create and a tremendous range of innovative and experimental methods have been devised and employed in recent years across and beyond the social sciences (Dowling, Lloyd and Suchet-Pearsohn 2017). *What is Rhythmanalysis?* seeks to contribute to this effort. Rhythmanalysis as envisaged by Lefebvre and developed by others is not a single off-the-shelf method that can be utilized in a technical manner. And this text does not offer a prescriptive set of instructions that can be applied regardless of context and research questions. Rhythmanalysis is more of an 'inventive' (Lury and Wakeford 2012) approach or a source for inventive thinking (McCormack 2013: 73) which brings together a versatile set of techniques for their capacity to address specific questions related to the spacetimes of the everyday. As Kullman and Palludan write, 'one of the

---

[5] This is similar to the conscious kinaesthetic awareness of dance discussed in Chapter 1.

appeals of rhythmanalysis is its incomplete and open-ended character that makes the approach combinable with various styles of thinking and researching' (2011: 349). This book is both a resource to stimulate further interest and imagination in doing rhythmanalysis and a call to researchers to experiment with the different practices and possibilities rhythmanalysis proposes.

References

Adam, B. (1998) *Timescapes of Modernity, The Environment and Invisible Hazards*, London and New York: Routledge.
Adams, T. E., S. Holman Jones and C. Ellis (eds) (2014) *Autoethnography, Understanding Qualitative Research*, Oxford: Oxford University Press.
Alhadeff-Jones, M. (2017) *Time and the Rhythms of Emancipatory Education*, London and New York: Routledge.
Alvarez, D. (2007) 'The return of Henri Lefebvre', *Grand Valley Review*, 31(1), Article 19: 51–74.
Amin, A., and N. Thrift (2002) *Cities: Reimagining the Urban*, Cambridge: Polity.
Anderson, B. (2009) 'Affective atmospheres', *Emotion, Space and Society*, 2: 77–81.
Anim-Addo, A. (2014) '"The great event of the fortnight": Steamship rhythms and colonial communication', *Mobilities*, 9(3): 369–83.
Apperley, T. (2010) *Gaming Rhythms: Play and Counterplay from the Situated to the Global*, Amsterdam: Institute of Network Cultures.
Ash, J., and L. Gallacher (2015) 'Becoming attuned: Objects, affects and embodied methodology' in M. Perry and C. L. Medina (eds) *Methodologies of Embodiment, Inscribing Bodies in Qualitative Research*, Abingdon, Oxon: Routledge.
Atkinson, P. (2015) *For Ethnography*, London: Sage.
Bachelard, G. (1964) *Poetics of Space*, Boston, MA: Beacon Press.
Bachelard, G. (2000 [1931]) in R. Durie (ed.) *Time & the Instant, Essays in the Physics and Philosophy of Time*, Manchester: Clinamen Press.
Back, L. (2007) *The Art of Listening*, Oxford: Berg.
Back, L. (2012) 'Live sociology: Social research and its futures' in L. Back and N. Puwar (eds) *Live Methods*, Oxford: Wiley-Blackwell/The Sociological Review.
Back, L., and N. Puwar (eds) (2012) *Live Methods*, Oxford: Wiley-Blackwell/The Sociological Review.

Barrows, A. (2016) *Time, Literature and Cartography after the Spatial Turn, The Chronometric Imaginary*, New York: Palgrave Macmillan US.

Bates, C. (ed.) (2015) *Video Methods, Social Science Research in Motion*, Abingdon: Routledge.

Bates, C., and A. Rhys-Taylor (eds) (2017) *Walking Through Social Research*, New York and Abingdon: Routledge.

Bennett, J. (2015) '"Snowed in!": Offbeat rhythms and belonging in everyday practice', *Sociology*, 49(5): 955–69.

Benveniste, E. (1966) *Problèmes de linguistique générale*, Paris: Gallimard.

Biddle, I., and M. Thompson (eds) (2013) *Sound, Music, Affect: Theorizing Sonic Experience*, London: Bloomsbury.

Birkin, M. (2018) 'Big data: Big data for social science research', *Ubiquity*, 1: 1–7.

Bissell, D., and G. Fuller (eds) (2011) *Stillness in a Mobile World*, London and New York: Routledge.

Blomley, N. (2007) 'How to turn a beggar into a bus stop: Law, traffic and the "Function of the place"', *Urban Studies*, 44(9): 1697–712.

Blue, S. (2017) 'Institutional rhythms: Combining practice theory and rhythmanalysis to conceptualise processes of institutionalisation', *Time & Society*, 0(0): 1–29.

Böhme, G. (1993) 'Atmosphere as the fundamental concept of a new aesthetics', *Thesis Eleven*, 36: 113–26.

Borch, C. (2005) 'Urban imitations: Tarde's sociology revisited', *Theory, Culture and Society*, 22(3): 81–100.

Borch, C., and A.-C. Lange (2017) 'High-frequency trader subjectivity: Emotional attachment and discipline in an era of algorithms', *Socio-Economic Review*, 15(2): 283–306.

Borch, C., K. Bondo Hansen and A.-C. Lange (2015) 'Markets, bodies, and rhythms: A rhythmanalysis of financial markets from open-outcry trading to high-frequency trading', *Environment and Planning D*, 33(6): 1080–97.

Bourdain, A. (2000) *Kitchen Confidential, Adventures in the Culinary Underbelly*, London: Bloomsbury.

Bull, M. (2000) *Sounding Out the City: Personal Stereos and the Management of Everyday Life*, Oxford: Berg.

Butler, C. (2012) *Henri Lefebvre, Spatial Politics, Everyday Life and the Right to the City*, Abingdon, Oxon: Routledge.

Chen, Y. (2013) '"Walking with": A Rhythmanalysis of London's East End', *Culture Unbound*, 3: 531–49.

Chen, Y. (2017) *Practising Rhythmanalysis, Theories and Methodologies*, London and New York: Roman and Littlefield.

Clark, A., and N. Emmel (2010) 'Using walking interviews', Realities Toolkit #13, NCRM: http://eprints.ncrm.ac.uk/1323/1/13-toolkit-walking-interviews.pdf

Clough, P. T., K. Gregory, B. Haber and R. J. Scannell (2015) 'The datalogical turn' in P Vannini, (ed.) *Non-Representational Methodologies: Re-Envisioning Research*, London: Routledge.

Cook, M., and T. Edensor (2017) 'Cycling through dark space: Apprehending landscape otherwise', *Mobilities*, 12(1): 1–19.

Cowan, M. (2012) *Technology's Pulse: Essays on Rhythm in German Modernism*, London: Institute of Germanic and Romance Studies, School of Advanced Study, University of London.

Cox, R., A. Irving and C. Wright (eds) (2016) *Beyond Text?: Critical Practices and Sensory Anthropology*, Manchester: Manchester University Press.

Crang, M. (2001) 'Rhythms of the city, temporalised space and motion' in J. May and N. Thrift (eds) *Timespace, Geographies of Temporality*, London and New York: Routledge.

Crang, M. (2003) 'Qualitative methods: Touchy feeling, look-see?', *Progress in Human Geography*, 27(4): 494–504.

Crang, M. (2005) 'Time: Space' in P. Cloke and R. Johnston (eds) *Spaces of Geographical Thought, Deconstructing Human Geography's Binaries*, London: Sage.

Crary, J. (2013) *24/7, Late Capitalism and the Ends of Sleep*, London and New York: Verso.

Crawford, M. (2010) *Shop Class as Soulcraft: An Inquiry Into the Value of Work*, London: Penguin.

Crespi, P. (2014) 'Rhythmanalysis in gymnastics and dance: Rudolf Bode and Rudolf Laban', *Body & Society*, 20(3 and 4): 30–50.

Creswell, T. (2006) *On the Move, Mobility in the Modern Western World*, Abingdon, Oxon and New York: Routledge.

Cronin, A. M. (2006) 'Advertising and the metabolism of the city: Urban spaces, commodity rhythms', *Environment and Planning D: Society and Space*, 24(4): 615–32.

Davies, W. (2018) 'The political economy of pulse: Techno-somatic rhythm and real-time data', *Ephemera* 18(4): http://www.ephemerajournal.org/

De Certeau, M. (1984) *The Practice of Everyday Life*, Berkeley, CA: University of California Press.

Degen, M. M. (2008) *Sensing Cities, Regenerating Public Life in Barcelona and Manchester*, London and New York; Routledge.

Degen, M. M. (2010) 'Consuming urban rhythms: Let's Ravalejar' in T. Edensor (ed.) *Geographies of Rhythm: Nature, Place, Mobilities and Bodies*, Farnham: Ashgate.

Degen, M., C. DeSilvey and G. Rose (2008) 'Experiencing visualities in designed urban environments: Learning from Milton Keynes', *Environment and Planning A*, 40(8): 1901–20.

Deleuze, G., and F. Guattari (1987) *A Thousand Plateaus, Capitalism and Schizophrenia*, London and New York: Bloomsbury.

DeLyser, D., and S. Sui (2012) 'Crossing the qualitative-quantitative divide II', *Progress in Human Geography*, Online First.

Demetry, D. (2013) 'Regimes of meaning: The intersection of space and time in kitchen cultures', *Journal of Contemporary Ethnography*, 42(5): 576–607.

Denzin, N. K., and Y. S. Lincoln (2018, 5th edition) 'Introduction: The discipline and practice of qualitative research' in N. K. Denzin and Y. S. Lincoln (eds) *The SAGE Handbook of Qualitative Research*, London: Sage: 1–26.

Dey, P., L. Marti, S. Teasdale and P. Seanor (2016) 'Alternative enterprises, rhythms and (post)capitalism: Mapping spatio-temporal practices of reproduction, escape and intervention', *Conference Paper: 32nd European Group for Organizational Studies (EGOS) Colloquium, Sub-theme 57: Making Utopias Real: Social Innovation, Movements and Change*, Naples, 7–9 July.

Dixon, D. P., and E. R. Straughan (2010) 'Geographies of touch/touched by geography', *Geography Compass*, 4(5): 449–59.

Dowling, R., K. Lloyd and S. Suchet-Pearson (2017) 'Qualitative methods 3: Experimenting, picturing, sensing', *Progress in Human Geography*, Online First, 40: 1–10.

Duffy, M., G. Waitt and T. Harada (2016) 'Making sense of sound: Visceral sonic mapping as a research tool', *Emotion, Space and Society*, 20: 49–57.

Duffy, M., G. Waitt, A. Gorman-Murray and C. Gibson (2011) 'Bodily rhythms: Corporeal capacities to engage with festival spaces', *Emotion, Space and Society*, 4: 17–24.

Edensor, T. (2000) 'Moving through the city' in D. Bell and A. Haddour (eds) *City Visions*, Harlow: Pearson Education Limited.

Edensor, T. (2006) 'Reconsidering national temporalities, institutional times, everyday routines, serial spaces and synchronicities', *European Journal of Social Theory*, 9(4): 525–45.

Edensor, T. (2008) 'Walking through ruins' in T. Ingold and J. L. Vergunst (eds) *Ways of Walking, Ethnography and Practice on Foot*, Aldershot: Ashgate.

Edensor, T. (2010a) 'Introduction: Thinking about rhythm and space' in T. Edensor (ed.) *Geographies of Rhythm: Nature, Place, Mobilities and Bodies*, Farnham: Ashgate.

Edensor, T. (2010b) 'Walking in rhythms: Place, regulation, style and the flow of experience' *Visual Studies*, 25(1): 69–79.

Edensor, T. (2011) 'Commuter: Mobility, rhythm and commuting' in T. Creswell and P. Merriman (eds) *Geographies of Mobilities: Practices, Spaces, Subjects*, Farnham: Ashgate.

Edensor, T. (2014) 'Rhythm and arrhythmia' in P. Adey, D. Bissell, K. Hannam, P. Merriman and M. Sheller (eds) *The Routledge Handbook of Mobilities*, Abingdon, Oxon: Routledge.

Edensor, T., and C. Bowdler (2015) 'Site-specific dance: Revealing and contesting the ludic qualities, everyday rhythms, and embodied habits of place', *Environment and Planning A*, 47: 709–26.

Edensor, T., and J. Holloway (2008) 'Rhythmanalysing the coach tour: The ring of kerry, Ireland', *Transactions of the Institute of British Geographers*, 33: 483–501.

Edensor, T., and J. Larsen (2017) 'Rhythmanalysing marathon running: "A drama of rhythms"', *Environment and Planning A*, 0(0): 1–17, Online First.

Edensor, T., M. Kärrholm and J. Wirdelöv (2017) 'Rhythmanalysing the urban runner: Pildammsparken, Malmö', *Applied Mobilities*, Online First: 1–18.

Elden, S. (2004a) *Understanding Henri Lefebvre, Theory and the Possible*, London and New York: Continuum.

Elden, S. (2004b) 'Rhythmanalysis: An introduction' in H. Lefebvre (ed.), *Rhythmanalysis: Space, Time and Everyday Life*, London: Continuum International Publishing Group Ltd.

Elden, S. (2006) 'Some are born posthumously: The French afterlife of Henri Lefebvre', *Historical Materialism*, 14(4): 185–202.

Elden, S., E. Lebas and E. Kofman (eds) (2017) *Henri Lefebvre, Key writings*, London: Bloomsbury Academic.

Elliott, D., and D. Culhane (eds) *A Different Kind of Ethnography, Imaginative Practices and Creative Methodologies*, Toronto: University of Toronto Press.

Evans, J. (2010) 'Re-thinking catastrophe in the time of climate change' in T. Edensor (ed.) *Geographies of Rhythm: Nature, Place, Mobilities and Bodies*, Farnham: Ashgate.

Evans, J., and P. Jones (2008) 'Towards Lefebvrian socio-nature? A film about rhythm, nature and science', *Geography Compass*, 2/3: 659–70.

Evans, J., and P. Jones (2011) 'The walking interview: Methodology, mobility and place', *Applied Geography*, 31(2): 849–58.

Evans, R., and A. Franklin (2010) 'Equine beats: Unique rhythms (and floating harmony) of horses and riders' in T. Edensor (ed.) *Geographies of Rhythm: Nature, Place, Mobilities and Bodies*, Farnham: Ashgate.

Fine, G. A. (1996) *Kitchens, The Culture of Restaurant Work*, Berkeley and Los Angeles: University of California.

Flaherty, M. G. (2011) *The Textures of Time, Agency and Temporal Experience*, Philadelphia: Temple University Press.

Foucault, M. (1975) *Discipline and Punish: The Birth of the Prison*, New York: Random House.

Freeman, E. (2010) *Time Binds: Queer Temporalities, Queer Histories*, Durham, NC: Duke University Press.

Gallagher, M., and J. Prior (2014) 'Sonic geographies: Exploring phonographic methods', *Progress in Human Geography*, 38(2): 267–84.

Garrett, B. L., and H. Hawkins (2015) 'Creative video ethnographies: Video methodologies of urban exploration' in C. Bates (ed.) *Video Methods, Social Science Research in Motion*, Abingdon: Routledge.

Gherardi, S. (1996) 'Gendered organizational cultures: Narratives of women travellers in a male world', *Gender, Work & Organization* 3(4): 187–201.

Gibas, P. (2013) 'Uncanny underground: Absences, ghosts and the rhythmed everyday of the Prague metro', *cultural geographies*, 20(4): 485–500.

Gibbs, A. (2015) 'Writing as method: Attunement, resonance and rhythm' in B. T. Knudsen and C. Stage (eds) *Affective Methodologies, Developing Cultural Research Strategies for the Study of Affect*, London: Palgrave Macmillan.

Goffman, E. (1959) *The Presentation of Self in Everyday Life*, London: Penguin Books.

Graham, J. (2015) 'Rhythmanalysis: The line as a record of the *moving present*', *Journal of Visual Art Practice*, 14(1): 54–71.

Graham, S. (2014) 'Disruptions' in P. Adey, D. Bissell, K. Hannam, P. Merriman and M. Sheller (eds) *The Routledge Handbook of Mobilities*, Abingdon, Oxon: Routledge.

Grasseni, C. (2004) 'Skilled vision. An apprenticeship in breeding aesthetics', *Social Anthropology*, 12(1): 41–55.

Grimshaw, A. (2011) 'The Bellwether Ewe: Recent developments in ethnographic filmmaking and the aesthetics of anthropological enquiry', *Cultural Anthropology*, 26(2): 247–62.

Hägerstrand, T. (1970) 'What about people in regional science?', *Regional Science Association*, 24(1): 6–21.

Hall, T. (2010) 'Urban outreach and the polyrhythmic city' in T. Edensor (ed.) *Geographies of Rhythm: Nature, Place, Mobilities and Bodies*, Basingstoke: Ashgate.

Hall, T., and R. J. Smith (2014) 'Knowing the city: Maps, mobility and urban outreach work', *Qualitative Research*, 14(3): 294–310.

Hall, T., B. Lashua and A. Coffey (2008) 'Sound and the everyday in qualitative research', *Qualitative Inquiry*, 14(6): 1019–40.

Haraway, D. (1988) 'Situated knowledges: The science question in feminism and the privilege of partial perspective', *Feminist Studies*, 14(3): 575–99.

Harper, D. (2012) *Visual Sociology*, London: Routledge.

Harvey, D. (1973) *Social Justice and the City*, London: Arnold.

Harvey, M. (1999) 'Economies of time: A framework for analysing the restructuring of employment relations' in A. Felstead and N. Jewson (eds) *Global Trends in Flexible Labour*, Basingstoke: Macmillan Business.

Harvey, M., S. Quilley and H. Benyon (2002) *Exploring the Tomato, Transformations of Nature, Society and Economy*, Cheltenham: Edward Elgar.

Henriques, J., M. Tianen and P. Väliaho (2014) 'Rhythm returns: Movement and cultural theory', *Body & Society*, 20(3 and 4): 3–29.

Highmore, B. (2002) '*Street Life in London*: Towards a rhythmanalysis of London in the late nineteenth century', *New Formations*, 47: 171–93.

Hockey, J., and J. Allen-Collinson (2009) 'The sensorium at work: The sensory phenomenology of the working body', *The Sociological Review*, 57(2): 217–39.

Hollway, W., and T. Jefferson (2013, 2nd edition) *Doing Qualitative Research Differently, A Psychosocial Approach*, London: Sage.

Hubbard, P., and K. Lilley (2004) 'Pacemaking the modern city: The urban politics of speed and slowness', *Environment and Planning D: Society and Space*, 22(2): 273–94.

Hui, A. (2013) 'Moving with practices: The discontinuous, rhythmic and material mobilities of leisure', *Social & Cultural Geography* 14(8): 888–908.

Hunt, M. (2014) 'Urban photography/cultural geography: Spaces, objects, events', *Geography Compass*, 8(3): 151–68.
Ikoniadou, E. (2014) *The Rhythm Event, Art, Media and the Sonic*, Cambridge, MA and London: The MIT Press.
Ingold, T. (2000) *The Perception of the Environment: Essays in Livelihood, Dwelling, and Skill*, London: Routledge.
Ingold, T. (2011) *Being Alive: Essays on Movement, Knowledge and Description*, Routledge: London.
Ingold, T., and J. L. Vergunst (2008) *Ways of Walking, Ethnography and Practice on Foot*, Farnham: Ashgate.
Jones, O. (2011) 'Lunar-solar rhythmpatterns: Towards the material cultures of tides', *Environment and Planning A*, 43(10): 2285–303.
Jones, P., and S. Warren (2016) 'Time, rhythm and the creative economy', *Transactions of the Institute of British Geographers*, 41: 286–96.
Jungnickel, K. (2015) 'Jumps, stutters, blurs and other failed images: Using time-lapse video in cycling research' in C. Bates (ed.) *Video Methods, Social Science Research in Motion*, Abingdon: Routledge.
Karina, L., and M. Kant (2004) *Hitler's Dancers: German Modern Dance and the Third Reich*, New York: Berghahn.
Kärrholm, M. (2009) 'To the rhythm of shopping – On synchronisation in urban landscapes of consumption', *Social & Cultural Geography*, 10(4): 421–40.
Kerfoot, D., and D. Knights (1993) 'Management, masculinity and manipulation: From paternalism to corporate strategy in financial services in Britain', *Journal of Management Studies*, 30(4): 659–79.
Kern, L. (2015) 'Rhythms of gentrification: Eventfulness and slow violence in a happening neighbourhood', *cultural geographies*, 23(3): 414–57.
King, A., and M. de Rond (2011) 'Boat race: Rhythm and the possibility of collective performance', *The British Journal of Sociology*, 62(4): 565–85.
Kipfer, S., and K. Goonewardena (2013) 'Urban Marxism and the postcolonial question: Henri Lefebvre and "colonisation"', *Historical Materialism*, 21(2): 1–41.
Knowles, C. (2014) *Flip Flop, A Journey Through Globalisation's Backroads*, London: Pluto Press.
Knudsen, B. T. and C. Stage (eds) (2015) *Affective Methodologies, Developing Cultural Research Strategies for the Study of Affect*, London: Palgrave Macmillan.
Korczynski, M. (2014) *Songs of the Factory*, Ithaca: ILR Press.

Korczynski, M., M. Pickering and E. Robertson (2013) *Rhythms of Labour: Music at Work in Britain*, Cambridge: Cambridge University Press.

Kullman, K., and C. Palludan (2011) 'Rhythmanalytical sketches: Agencies, school journeys, temporalities', *Children's Geographies*, 9(3–4): 347–59.

Kusenbach, M. (2003) 'Street phenomenology: The go-along as ethnographic research tool', *Ethnography*, 4(3): 455–85.

Laban, R. (2011 [nd]) 'Answers to ten questions on industrial rhythm' in D. McCaw (ed.) *The Laban Sourcebook*, London and New York: Routledge.

Laban, R. (2014 [1921]) 'Eurhythmy and Kakorhythmy in art and education', *Body & Society*, 20(3 and 4): 75–8.

Laban, R., and F. C. Lawrence (1947) *Effort*, London: Macdonald & Evans.

LaBelle, B. (2008) 'Pump up the bass – Rhythm, cars and auditory scaffolding', *Senses & Society*, 3(2): 187–204.

LaBelle, B. (2010) *Acoustic Territories, Sound Culture and Everyday Life*, London: Bloomsbury.

Lahad, K., and V. May (2017) 'Just one? solo dining, gender and temporal belonging in public spaces', *Sociological Research Online*, 22(2), 12: http://www.socresonline.org.uk/22/2/12.html

Lange, A.-C. (2016) 'Organizational ignorance: An ethnographic study of high-frequency trading', *Economy and Society*, 45(2): 230–50.

Latham, A., and D. McCormack (2009) 'Thinking with images in non-representational cities: Vignettes from Berlin', *Area*, 41(3): 252–62.

Law, J., and J. Urry (2004) 'Enacting the social', *Economy and Society*, 33(3): 390–410.

Lefebvre, H. (1959) *La Somme et le Reste, Tomes I & II*, Paris: La Nef de Paris.

Lefebvre, H. (1991 [1974]) *The Production of Space*, Oxford: Wiley-Blackwell.

Lefebvre, H. (1995 [1968]) *Writings on Cities*, Oxford: Wiley-Blackwell.

Lefebvre, H. (2004 [1992]) *Rhythmanalysis: Space, Time and Everyday Life*, London: Continuum International Publishing Group Ltd.

Lefebvre, H. (2012 [1962]) *Introduction to Modernity*, London: Verso.

Lefebvre, H. (2014a [1947, 1961, 1981]) *Critique of Everyday Life, The One-Volume Edition*, London and New York: Verso.

Lefebvre, H. (2014b) *Toward an Architecture of Enjoyment*, Minneapolis and London: University of Minnesota Press.

Lefebvre, H. (2016 [1968]) *Everyday Life in the Modern World*, London and New York: Bloomsbury.

Lefebvre, H., and C. Levich (1987) 'The everyday and everydayness', *Yale French Studies*, 73: 7–11.

Lefebvre, H., and C. Régulier (2004a [1985]) 'The rhythmanalytical project' in H. Lefebvre (ed.), *Rhythmanalysis*, London: Continuum International Publishing Group Ltd.

Lefebvre, H., and C. Régulier (2004b [1986]) 'Attempt at the rhythmanalysis of Mediterranean cities' in H. Lefebvre (ed.) *Rhythmanalysis*, London: Continuum International Publishing Group Ltd.

Lefebvre, H., C. Régulier and M. Zayani (1999) 'The rhythmanalytical project', *Rethinking Marxism*, 11(1): 5–13.

Lury, C., and N. Wakeford (2012) *Inventive Methods: The Happening of the Social*, Abingdon: Routledge.

Lyon, D. (2012) 'The labour of refurbishment: The building and the body in space and time' in S. Pink, D. Tutt and A. Dainty (eds) *Ethnographic Research in the Construction Industry*, Abingdon, Oxon: Taylor and Francis.

Lyon, D. (2016) 'Doing audio-visual montage to explore time and space: The everyday rhythms of Billingsgate Fish Market', *Sociological Research Online*, 21(3), 12: http://www.socresonline.org.uk/21/3/12.html

Lyon, D., and L. Back (2012) 'Fish and fishmongers in a global city: Socio-economy, craft, and social relations on a London market', *Sociological Research Online*, 17(2): 23: http://www.socresonline.org.uk/17/2/23.html

MacKenzie, D. (2004) 'Social connectivities in global financial markets', *Environment and Planning D: Society and Space*, 22: 83–101.

Makagon, D., and M. Neumann (2008) *Recording Culture: Audio Documentary and the Ethnographic Experience*, London: Sage.

May, J., and N. Thrift (2001) *Timespace, Geographies of Temporality*, London and New York: Routledge.

McCormack, D. (2013) *Refrains for Moving Bodies*, Durham and London: Duke University Press.

McDowell, L. (1997) *Capital Culture: Gender at Work in the City*, Oxford: Blackwell.

McNeill, W. H. (1997) *Keeping Together in Time, Dance and Drill in Human History*, Cambridge, MA: Harvard University Press.

Meadows, R., S. Nettleton and J. Neale (2017) 'Sleep waves and recovery from drug and alcohol dependence: Towards a rhythm analysis of sleep in residential treatment', *Social Science & Medicine*, 184: 124–33.

Mels, T. (ed.) (2004) *Reanimating Places, A Geography of Rhythms*, Farnham: Ashgate.

Merchant, S. (2011) 'The body and the senses: Visual methods, videography and the submarine sensorium', *Body & Society*, 17(1): 53–71.

Merleau-Ponty, M. (2012 [1945]) *Phenomenology of Perception*, London and New York: Routledge.

Merrifield, A. (2000) 'Henri Lefebvre: A socialist in space' in M. Crang and N. Thrift (eds) *Thinking Space*, London and New York: Routledge.

Merrifield, A. (2006) *Henri Lefebvre, A Critical Introduction*, Abingdon: Routledge.

Meschonnic, H. (1982) *Critique du rythme: Anthropologie historique du langage*, Lagrasse: Verdier.

Michon, P. (2005) *Rythmes, pouvoir, mondialisation*, Paris: PUF.

Michon, P. (2011) 'A short history of rhythm since the 1970s', *Rhuthmos*: http://rhuthmos.eu/IMG/article_PDF/A-Short-History-of-Rhythm-Theory_a462.pdf [accessed 9 September 2017].

Michon, P. (2016) 'Could rhythm become a new scientific paradigm for the humanities?' *Conference: Rhythm as Pattern and Variation*, Goldsmiths: https://audioculture.net/2016/05/25/audio-rhythm-as-pattern-and-variation-political-social-artistic-inflections/ [accessed 15 September 2017].

Michon, P. (2017) 'Rhythm in the work of Emile Benveniste and Henri Meschonnic' CHASE seminar series, *Rhythmanalysis: Everything You Always Wanted to Know but Were Afraid to Ask*: http://generic.wordpress.soton.ac.uk/rhythmanalysis/seminar/ [accessed 15 September 2017].

Middleton, J. (2009) '"Stepping in time": Walking, time, and space in the city', *Environment and Planning A*, 41: 1943–61.

Middleton, J. (2010) 'Sense and the city: Exploring the embodied geographies of urban walking', *Social & Cultural Geography*, 11(6): 575–96.

Miller, J. (2010) *On the Move, Visualising Action*, London: Estorick Foundation.

Mitchell, C. (2011) *Doing Visual Research*, London: Sage.

Moore, R. (2013) 'The beat of the city: Lefebvre and rhythmanalysis', *Situations*, 5(1): 61–77.

Morris, E. (2017) *Rhythm in Acting and Performance, Embodied Approaches and Understandings*, London and New York: Bloomsbury Methuen Performance.

Mulíček, O., R. Osman and D. Seidenglanz (2015) 'Urban rhythms: A chronotopic approach to urban timespace', *Time & Society*, 24(3): 304–25.

Mylan and Southerton (2017) 'The social ordering of an everyday practice: The case of laundry', *Sociology*, 1–18.

Nancel, L. (2014) 'Situating reflexivity: Voices, positionalities and representations in feminist ethnographic texts', *Women's Studies International Forum*, 43: 75–83

Nansen, B., M. Arnold, M. R. Gibbs and H. Davis (2009) 'Domestic orchestration, Rhythms in the mediated home', *Time & Society*, 18(2/3): 181–207.

Neuhaus, F. (2010) 'UrbanDiary – A tracking project, capturing the beat and rhythm of the city: Using GPS devices to visualise individual and collective routines within Central London', *The Journal of Space Syntax*, 1(2): 2044–7507.

Norris, F. (1994 [1903]) *The Pit*, New York, NY: Penguin Group.

O'Connor, P. (2017) 'Rhythmanalysis as a tool in social analysis on ethnicity in Hong Kong', *Asian Ethnicity*, Online First: 1–15.

Obert, J. C. (2008) 'Sound and sentiment: A rhythmanalysis of television', *Continuum*, 22(3): 409–17.

Ocejo, R. E. (2017) *Masters of Craft, Old Job in the New Urban Economy*, Princeton and Oxford: Princeton University Press.

Okely, J. (1992) 'Anthropology and autobiography: Participatory experience and embodied knowledge' in J. Okely and H. Cathaway (eds) *Anthropology and Autobiography*, Abingdon: Routledge.

Okely, J. (2007) 'Fieldwork embodied', *The Sociological Review*, 55(S1): 65–79.

Orbach, S. (2016) *In Therapy: How Conversations with Psychotherapists Really Work*, London: Profile Books and Wellcome Collection.

Palmer, M., and O. Jones (2014) 'On breathing and geography: Explorations of data sonifications of timespace processes with illustrating examples for a tidally dynamic landscape (Severn Estuary, UK)', *Environment And Planning A*, 46: 222–40.

Parker, B. (2016) 'Feminist forays in the city: Imbalance and intervention in urban research methods', *Antipode*, 48(5): 1337–58.

Parkes, D., and N. Thrift (1979) 'Time spacemakers and entrainment', *Transactions of the Institute of British Geographers*, 4(3): 353–72.

Paterson, M. (2009) 'Haptic geographies: Ethnography, haptic knowledges and sensuous dispositions', *Progress in Human Geography*, 33(6): 766–88.

Peake, L. (2016) 'On feminism and feminist allies in knowledge production in urban geography', *Urban Geography*, 37(6): 830–8.

Pedwell, C., and A. Whitehead (2012) 'Affecting feminism: Questions of feeling in feminist theory', *Feminist Theory* 13(2): 115–29.

Perry, M., and C. L. Medina (eds) (2015) *Methodologies of Embodiment, Inscribing Bodies in Qualitative Research*, Abingdon, Oxon: Routledge.

Pettinger, L. (2017) 'Green collar work: Conceptualizing and exploring an emerging field of work', *Sociology Compass*, 11: 1–13.

Pierce, J., and M. Lawhon (2015) 'Walking as method: Toward methodological forthrightness and comparability in urban geographical research', *The Professional Geographer*, 67(4): 655–62.

Pink, S. (2005) *The Future of Visual Anthropology: Engaging the Senses*, London: Routledge.

Pink, S. (2007, 2nd edition) *Doing Visual Ethnography*, London: Sage

Pink, S., P. Hubbard, M. O'Neill and A. Radley (2010) 'Walking across disciplines: From ethnography to arts practice', *Visual Studies*, 25: 1–7.

Pink, S. (2015, 2nd edition) *Doing Sensory Ethnography*, London: Sage.

Poe, E. (2017) *Reset: My Fight for Inclusion and Lasting Change*, New York: Spiegel & Grau.

Potts, T. (2010) 'Life hacking and everyday rhythm' in T. Edensor (ed.) *Geographies of Rhythm: Nature, Place, Mobilities and Bodies*, Farnham: Ashgate.

Potts, T. (2015) 'Book review: Rhythmanalysis: Space, time and everyday life', *The Journal of Architecture*, 20(3): 550–4.

Pryke, M. (2000) 'Tracing economic rhythms through visual and audio montage', Faculty of Social Sciences, The Open University: http://www.open.ac.uk/socialsciences/berlin/ [accessed 29 February 2016].

Pryke, M. (2002) 'The white noise of capitalism: Audio and visual montage and sensing economic change', *cultural geographies*, 9: 472–7.

Redmon, D. (2015) 'Documentary criminology: Expanding the criminological imagination with "Mardi Gras- Made in China" as a case study', *Societies*, 5(2): 425–41.

Revill, G. (2013) 'Points of departure: Listening to rhythm in the sonorous spaces of the railway station', *The Sociological Review*, 61(S1): 51–68. Special Issue: 'Urban Rhythms, Mobilities, space and interaction in the contemporary city'.

Revol, C. (2012/3) 'Le succès de Lefebvre dans les *urban studies* Anglosaxonnes et les conditions de sa redécouverte en France', *L'Homme et la Société*, 185–6: 105–18.

Rose, G. (1993) *Feminism & Geography: The Limits of Geographical Knowledge*, Minneapolis: University of Minnesota Press.
Rose, G. (1997) 'Situating knowledges: Positionality, reflexivities and other tactics', *Progress in Human Geography*, 21(3): 305–20.
Rose, G. (2016, 4th edition) *Visual Methodologies: An Introduction to the Interpretation of Visual Materials*, London: Sage.
Rose, M. (2004) *The Mind at Work, Valuing the Intelligence of the American Worker*, London: Penguin Books.
Ross, K. (1997) 'Lefebvre on the situationists: An Interview', *October*, 79: 69–83.
Samuel, G. (2015) 'Introduction' in H. Leaper (ed.) *Sybil Andrews and the Grosvenor School Linocuts*, London: Osborne Samuel.
Schwanen, T., I. van Aalst, J. Brands and T. Timan (2012) 'Rhythms of the night: Spatiotemporal inequalities in the nighttime economy', *Environment and Planning A*, 44: 2064–85.
Sennett, R. (2009) *The Craftsman*, London: Penguin.
Sgibnev, W. (2015) 'Rhythms of being together: Public space in Urban Tajikistan through the lens of rhythmanalysis', *International Journal of Sociology and Social Policy*, 35(7/8): 533–49.
Sharma, S. (2014) *In the Meantime, Temporality and Cultural Politics*, Durham and London: Duke University Press.
Shaw, W. S., D. DeLyser and M. Crang (2015) 'Limited by imagination alone: Research methods in cultural geographies', *cultural geographies*, 22(2): 211–15.
Shields, R. (1998) *Lefebvre, Love and Struggle, Spatial Dialectics*, London: Routledge.
Shields, R. (2011, 2nd edition) 'Henri Lefebvre' in P. Hubbard and R. Kitchin (eds) *Key Thinkers on Space and Place*, London: Sage.
Simonsen, K. (2004) 'Spatiality, temporality and the construction of the city' in J. O. Bærenholdt and K. Simonsen (eds) *Space Odysseys, Spatiality and Social relations in the 21st Century*, Aldershot: Ashgate.
Simonsen, K. (2005) 'Bodies, sensations, space and time: The contribution of Henri Lefebvre', *Geografiska Annaler Series B Human Geography*, 87(1): 1–14.
Simpson, P. (2008) 'Chronic everyday life: Rhythmanalysing street performance', *Social & Cultural Geography*, 9(7): 807–29.
Simpson, P. (2012) 'Apprehending everyday rhythms: Rhythmanalysis, time-lapse photography, and the space-time of everyday street performance', *cultural geographies*, 19(4): 423–45.

Skeggs, B., and S. Yuill (2016) 'The methodology of a multi-model project examining how Facebook infrastructures social relations', *Information, Communication & Society*, 19(10): 1356–72.

Smith, R. J., and K. Hetherington (2013) 'Urban rhythms: Mobilities, space and interaction in the contemporary city' Introduction to Special Issue on Urban Rhythms, *The Sociological Review*, 61(1): 4–16.

Smith, R. J., and T. Hall (2013) 'No time out: Mobility, rhythmicity and urban patrol in the twenty-four hour city', *The Sociological Review*, 61: 89–108.

Snyder, B. (2016) *The Disrupted Workplace, Time and the Moral Order of Flexible Capitalism*, Oxford: Oxford University Press.

Soja, E. (2010) *Seeking Spatial Justice*, Minneapolis: University of Minnesota Press.

Solnit, R. (2003) *Motion Studies: Time, Space & Eadweard Muybridge*, London: Bloomsbury Publishing plc.

Solnit, R (2014) *Wanderlust: A History of Walking*, London: Granta.

Southerton, D. (2013) 'Habits, routines and temporalities of consumption: From individual behaviours to the reproduction of everyday practices', *Time & Society*, 22(3): 335–55.

Spalding, F. (2014) *Virginia Woolf: Art, Life and Vision*, London: National Portrait Gallery.

Spencer, S. (2011) *Visual Research Methods in the Social Sciences, Awakening Visions*, London: Routledge.

Spinney, J. (2010) 'Improvising rhythms: Re-reading urban time and space through everyday practices of cycling' in T. Edensor (ed.) *Geographies of Rhythm: Nature, Place, Mobilities and Bodies*, Basingstoke: Ashgate.

Stanek, L. (2011) *Henri Lefebvre on Space, Architecture, Urban Research and the Production of Theory*, Minneapolis: University of Minnesota Press.

Stewart, K. (2007) *Ordinary Affects*, Durham and London: Duke University Press.

Stratford, E. (2015) *Geographies, Mobilities, and Rhythms over the Life-Course*, Abingdon: Routledge.

Straughan, E., and D. Dixon (2014) 'Rhythm and mobility in the inner and outer hebrides: Archipelago as art-science research site', *Mobilities*, 9(3): 452–78.

Thompson, E. P. (1967) 'Time, work-discipline, and industrial capitalism', *Past & Present*, 38: 56–97.

Thompson, G. F. (2016) 'Time, trading and algorithms in financial sector security', *New Political Economy*: 1–11.

Thorpe, H. (2015) 'Natural disaster arrhythmia and action sports: The case of the Christchurch earthquake', *International Review for the Sociology of Sport*, 50(3): 301–25.

Thrift, N. (2007) *Non-representational Theory, Space, Politics, Affect*, London: Routledge.

Tinati, R., S. Halford, L. Carr and C. Pope (2014) 'Big data: Methodological challenges and approaches for sociological analysis', *Sociology*, 48(4): 663–81.

Trentmann, F. (2009) 'Disruption is normal, blackouts, breakdowns and the elasticity of everyday life' in E. Shove, F. Trentmann and R. Wilk (eds) *Time, Consumption and Everyday Life, Practice, Materiality and Culture*, Oxford and New York: Berg.

Turner, P. K., and K. M. Norwood (2013) 'Body of research: Impetus, instrument, and impediment', *Qualitative Inquiry*, 19(9): 696–711.

Urry, J. (2007) *Mobilities*, Cambridge: Polity.

Vannini, P. (2012a) 'In time, out of time, rhythmanalyzing ferry mobilities', *Time & Society*, 21(2): 241–69.

Vannini, P. (2012b) 'Public ethnography and multimodality: Research from the book to the web' in P Vannini (ed.) *Popularizing Research*, New York: Peter Lang.

Vannini, P. (ed.) (2015) *Non-Representational Methodologies: Re-Envisioning Research*, London: Routledge.

Vannini, P., and J. Taggart (2014) *Off the Grid, Re-assembling Domestic Life*, London: Routledge.

Villneuve, E. (2008) 'The urban experience of placelessness: Perceptual rhythms in George Perec's *Un homme qui dort*' in L. McMahon (ed.) *Rhythms: Essays in French Literature, Thought and Culture*, Oxford: Peter Lang.

Virilio, P. (1986 [1977]) *Speed and Politics: An Essay on Dromology*, New York: Columbia University Press.

Wajcman, J. (2015) *Pressed for Time, The Acceleration of Life in Digital Capitalism*, Chicago: University of Chicago Press.

Wajcman, J., and N. Dodd (eds) (2017) *The Sociology of Speed, Digital, Organizational and Social Temporalities*, Oxford: Oxford University Press.

Weizman, E. (2000) *<yellow> Rhythms A Roundabout for London*, Rotterdam: 010 Publishers.

Whyte, W. H. (1980) *The Social Life of Small Urban Spaces*, Washington, DC: Conservation Foundation.
Willis, P., and M. Trondman (2002) 'Manifesto for ethnography', *Cultural Studies <-> Critical Methodologies*, 2(3): 394–402.
Wills, W. J., A. M. Dickinson, A. Meah and F. Short (2016) 'Reflections on the use of visual methods in a qualitative study of domestic kitchen practices', *Sociology*, 50: 470–85.
Wolkowitz, C. (2006) *Bodies at Work*, London: Sage.
Woodward, S. (2016) 'Object interviews, material imaginings and "unsettling" methods: Interdisciplinary approaches to understanding materials and material culture' *Qualitative Research*, 16(4): 359–74.
Wright, M. W. (2010) 'Gender and geography II: Bridging the gap – feminist, queer, and the geographical imaginary', *Progress in Human Geography*, 34(1): 56–66.
Wunderlich, F. M. (2008) 'Walking and rhythmicity: Sensing urban space', *Journal of Urban Design*, 13(1): 31–44.
Wunderlich, F. M. (2010) 'The aesthetics of place-temporality in everyday urban space: The case of Fitzroy Square' in T. Edensor (ed.) *Geographies of Rhythm: Nature, Place, Mobilities and Bodies*, Farnham: Ashgate.
Wunderlich, F. M. (2013) 'Place-temporality and urban place-rhythms in urban analysis and design: An aesthetic akin to music', *Journal of Urban Design*, 18(3): 383–408.
Zaloom, C. (2003) 'Ambiguous numbers: Trading technologies and interpretation in financial markets', *American Ethnologist*, 30(2): 258–72.
Zaloom, C. (2006) *Out of the Pits: Traders and Technology from Chicago to London*, Chicago, IL: University of Chicago Press.
Zerubavel, E. (1981) *Hidden Rhythms, Schedules and Calendars in Social Life*, Berkeley, CA: University of California Press.

Index

accelerating, acceleration 4, 67.
　See also speed
affect(s), affective 9, 49, 51,
　57, 60, 71, 81, 84, 90, 92, 99.
　See also emotion
algorithm(s), algorhythmic,
　algorhythmization 45, 61,
　62–4, 76, 89
alienating, alienation 12, 13,
　41, 49
Alvarez, D. 12, 15, 21, 102
Alys, F. 47
Andrews, S. 9
architecture 33, 50, 59, 68, 73
arrhythmia, arrhythmic 16,
　25–7, 34, 43, 50, 54
Ash, J. 84
atmosphere(s) 47, 51, 58, 68, 72,
　82, 84, 96, 99
audiovisual 16, 46, 65–76, 79,
　80, 91. See also film; video
auditory 31, 40. See also aural;
　listening; noise; sound
aural 31, 93. See also auditory;
　listening; noise; sound
autoethnographic,
　autoethnography 45,
　48, 53, 54, 56, 57.
　See also ethnography

Bachelard, G. 20, 22, 37
Back, L. 2, 51, 66, 74, 82, 90, 103
Barrows, A. 10, 14
Bennett, J. 43
Bergson, H. 20
Billingsgate 2, 14, 67–76, 80, 85,
　95, 101
biological, biology 22, 25–7, 34,
　35, 81
Blue, S. 34, 36, 85
Bode, R. 8
Bondo Hansen, K. 5, 16, 35, 40,
　41, 45, 58–65, 68, 76, 79, 89
Borch, C. 5, 16, 35, 40, 41, 45,
　58–65, 68, 76, 79, 89
Bowdler, C. 56–8
Bull, M. 39, 40, 82
Butler, C. 15, 21

calibrated, calibration 45,
　60, 61, 63, 76, 100.
　See also recalibration
camera(s) 8, 54, 66, 69,
　82, 87, 91, 92. See also
　photography; visual
capital, capitalism, capitalist 4,
　13, 16, 25, 26, 33, 34, 39, 40,
　41, 45, 47, 59, 60, 62, 64, 65,
　66, 76, 77, 86, 89, 102

car travel   30, 32, 47, 49, 55, 87, 92
Castaing-Taylor, L.   91
Chaplin, C.   65
Chen, Y.   5, 11, 21, 36–7, 39, 61, 83, 89
class   16, 27, 49, 68
clock-time   1, 40, 41, 69, 71, 75, 99
coach travel   38, 49, 50–3
colonization   13, 64, 77
Cook, M.   38, 53–5, 76
coordination   2, 25, 27, 58, 73, 77, 84, 86, 98, 100
Crang, M.   11, 13, 71, 81, 85, 103
cultural history   19, 36–7
cyclical rhythm(s), cyclical time   1, 12, 16, 24–6, 35, 40, 54, 63, 64, 75, 77, 85, 98, 102
cycling, cyclist   38, 46, 53–5, 76

dance, dancing   8, 23, 38, 46, 56–8, 87
Debord, G.   12, 20
Degen, M.   39–40, 83, 87
Deller, J.   47–8
DeLyser, D.   31, 88, 103
Demetry, D.   96, 100
DeSilvey, C.   87
desynchronization   41. *See also* synchronic
diary, diaries   37, 41, 43, 53, 54, 55, 76, 83, 89
disciplinary, discipline, disciplining   7, 27, 35, 40, 48, 100, 103

disrupt(s), disruption, disruptive   36, 43, 48, 50, 56, 76, 79, 86–8
Dos Santos, L.   22
dressage   16, 25, 27, 38, 41, 47, 54, 74
Duffy, M.   39, 83, 92
duration   20, 31, 32, 38, 46, 71, 73, 85, 100

Edensor, T.   4, 11, 13, 14, 16, 26, 37–9, 45–58, 67, 76, 79, 81, 84, 87
Elden, S.   2, 12, 13, 14, 21, 22, 32, 38
emotion, emotive   63, 81, 82, 92, 99, 100. *See also* affect
ethnicity   27, 48. *See also* race
ethnographic, ethnography   2, 5, 32, 37, 39, 40, 41, 60, 66, 67, 71, 80, 85, 88, 91, 92, 95, 99. *See also* observation; participant observation
ethnomethodology   87
eurhythmia, eurhythmic, eurhythmically   16, 25–7, 31, 34, 47, 55, 59
Eurhythmics   7
Evans, J.   37, 66, 93, 103

feminism, feminist   11, 15, 80, 81
ferry travel   38
festival   20–1, 39, 83
film   11, 54, 56–8, 65, 66, 68–76, 87, 91. *See also* audiovisual; video
financial traders, professionals   41, 58–65, 86. *See also* high frequency trade

Index

Fine, G. 99–100
Foucault, M. 7, 27

Gallacher, L. 84
gender, gendered 15, 16, 27, 35, 39, 48, 49, 64, 86
Gibbs, A. 90–1
Gilbreth, F. & L. 9

Hägerstrand, T. 11, 89
Hall, T. 4, 66, 69, 85
Harada, T. 92
Harvey, D. 21
Harvey, M. 86
Henriques, J. 3, 6, 9, 36, 85, 102, 103
Hetherington, K. 5, 16, 39
high frequency trade, traders, trading, HFT 45, 59, 61–5, 75, 76, 79, 89. *See also* financial traders
Highmore, B. 4, 36, 39
Hockney, D. 91
Holloway, J. 13, 38, 50, 52

immerse, immersion, immersive 30, 31, 32, 45, 57, 59, 60, 63, 66, 68, 69, 71, 80, 91
immobility 23, 32, 73. *See also* stillness
industrial, industrialization, industrialized 6, 7, 9, 12, 25, 26, 40, 41
isorhythmia 16, 25–7

Jaques-Dalcroze, J. 7, 8
Jones, O. 43, 92–3
Jones, P. 37, 41, 66, 93

Kärrholm, M. 38, 39, 53, 55
kinaesthetic 8, 80, 82. *See also* mobility
Kullman, K. 38, 80, 81, 103–4

Laban, R. 8, 9
LaBelle, B. 39, 40, 82
Lange, C. 5, 16, 35, 40, 41, 45–46, 58–65, 68, 76, 79, 89
Larsen, J. 38, 53–5
Latham, A. 66, 87
Lefebvre, H.
  balcony 27, 32, 60, 66, 68
  biography and politics 11–14
  Critique of Everyday Life 13–14, 19, 21, 23, 24, 26, 65
  Mediterranean Cities 33
  moments 19–21, 23, 34, 40, 54, 86
  The Production of Space 21, 23
  with Régulier, C. 25, 26, 27, 29, 33, 86, 102
  Rue Rambuteau 27, 29–30
light(s) 26, 32, 72–3
linear rhythm(s), linear time, linearity, linearization 1, 4, 13, 14, 16, 20, 24–6, 29, 34, 35, 40, 50, 54, 55, 63, 64, 71, 75, 77, 83, 86, 91, 98, 102, 103
listen, listening 7, 26, 30–2, 40, 66, 80, 82–3, 92
Long, R. 47
lorry drivers 41. *See also* truck drivers
Lyon, D. 2, 40, 41, 46, 67–76, 85

McCormack, D. 5, 7, 8, 9, 15, 31, 32, 34, 35, 56, 66, 80, 85, 87, 102, 103
McNeil, W. 27, 103
Marey, E.-J. 8, 9
markets
  finance 45, 58–65
  fish 2, 14, 16, 46, 67–76, 79, 80, 85, 91, 101
Marxism, Marxist(s) 13, 14, 23
material(s), materiality 10, 17, 22, 37, 45, 47–9, 54, 58, 59, 64, 65, 71, 74, 79, 80–2, 100
Mels, T. 5
Merrifield, A. 2, 5, 12, 13, 14, 15, 20, 21, 30, 34, 74
Meschonnic, H. 7, 91
metronome, metronomic 31, 45, 60, 61, 66
Michon, P. 7, 11
Middleton, J. 37
mobility, mobilities 9, 16, 19, 36, 37–8, 43, 46–58, 72, 76, 102. See also kinaesthetic
Muybridge, E. 8

narrative(s) 45, 48, 50, 51, 75, 76, 84, 100
natural, nature 12, 19, 25–7, 32, 36, 43, 47, 50, 53, 66, 73, 74, 98
noise(s), noisy 26, 30, 32, 60, 65, 66, 67, 74, 100
non-human 36, 43, 48, 93
Norris, F. 60

observation(s) 5, 9, 23, 37, 43, 53, 55, 60–2, 67, 90, 99, 100. See also ethnography; participation observation
olfactory 83. See also smell

Palludan, C. 38, 80, 81, 103–4
Palmer, M. 43, 92, 93
Paravel, V. 91
participant observation 34. See also ethnography; observation
Perec, G. 10–11
phenomenology, phenomenological 30, 31, 61
photograph(s), photography, photographer 8–9, 36, 37, 46, 50, 67–9, 72, 76, 87–8, 92. See also camera; visual
Pink, S. 37, 51, 66, 82, 91
polyrhythmia, polyrhythmic, polyrhythmically 8, 16, 25–7, 31, 32, 39, 58, 66, 68, 71, 75, 95, 97
power 13, 14, 19, 49, 87, 100, 102
Pryke, M. 66, 73
psychoanalysis, psychoanalyst 23, 83, 84

quantitative 5, 11, 31, 88

race 16. See also ethnicity
rail travel 38, 54, 84
recalibration(s) 41, 90, 100. See also calibration
Redmon, D. 91
reflexive(ly) 49, 51, 53, 55, 58, 61, 81, 84

refrain 84
repetition(s), repetitive 3, 4, 20, 21, 24–7, 39, 43, 47, 48, 50, 54, 73, 75, 91, 102
Revill, G. 35, 38, 83, 88
revolutionary, revolution(s) 13, 15, 20, 21, 40
Rose, G. 11, 82, 87
Rose, M. 97–8
running 38, 46, 53–5
rural landscape, life 12, 20, 25, 50, 54

Sables, W. 56–7, 58
schedule(s) 1, 26, 53, 63
seasonal, season(s) 12, 25, 26, 53, 75, 91–2, 97
Sharma, S. 4, 40, 41, 71, 73, 77, 100
Shaw, W. 103
Shields, R. 4, 14, 15, 19, 20
Simonsen, K. 35, 89
Simpson, P. 14, 34–5, 39, 40, 67–9, 71, 75
Situationism, Situationists 12, 20
Skeggs, B. 89
slow, slower, slowing, slowness 4, 6, 21, 38, 64, 65, 67, 74, 97
smell 54, 83, 91. See also olfactory
Smith, R. 5, 16, 39, 85
Snyder, B. 40, 41, 53, 76, 86, 90
sonic 80, 82, 92. See also sonification; sound
sonification(s) 43, 93
sound(s), soundscape, soundwalking 2, 32, 35, 39, 40, 46, 47, 50, 53, 55, 58, 65–7, 69, 71–4, 76, 82–3, 87, 91–3. See also auditory; aural; noise; sonification
spacetime(s) 7, 35, 84, 86, 103. See also timespace
spectral 23, 92
speed(s) 4, 8, 9, 31, 37, 38, 41, 47, 55, 62–4, 71, 74, 100. See also acceleration
Stewart, K. 90
still, stillness 4, 30, 32, 38, 41, 56–7, 69, 72, 73, 82, 87, 90. See also immobility
Stratford, E. 5, 36, 102
Sui, S. 31, 88
synchronic, synchronicity, synchronize(d), synchronizing, synchronization 11, 26, 36, 43, 47, 49, 50, 55, 58, 71, 74, 79, 86, 98, 99. See also desynchronization

Taylor, F. 8–9
Thorpe, H. 43
Thrift, N. 38, 39, 74, 75, 81, 85
Tianen, M. 3, 6, 9, 36, 85, 102, 103
time and motion studies 8, 9, 40
time-geography 11, 89
time-lapse 46, 67–76
timespace 37. See also spacetime
truck driver(s) 86, 90. See also lorry drivers

urban, urbanist, urbanized 2, 3, 5, 11, 12, 21, 25, 33, 36, 38–40, 48, 53, 55, 56, 59, 66, 73, 82, 83, 85, 87, 89

Vannini, P.   38, 51, 73, 91
Väliaho, P.   3, 6, 9, 36, 85, 102, 103
video   41, 57, 67, 71, 87, 91–2. See also audiovisual; film
visual, visualizations   2, 40, 50, 52–53, 58, 66, 67, 71, 80, 82, 89, 90, 92. See also camera; photography

Waitt, G.   92

walking   37–8, 46–9, 51, 57, 69, 72, 80
Warren, S.   37, 41, 66, 93
weather   43, 50, 54, 63, 75
Wirdelöv, J.   38, 53, 55
Woolf, V.   10
working rhythms   2, 8–9, 36, 40–41, 67–76, 95–102
Wunderlich, F.   37, 48, 92

Yuill, S.   89

www.ingramcontent.com/pod-product-compliance
Lightning Source LLC
Chambersburg PA
CBHW050832160426
43192CB00010B/1990